SO-AFV-797

Emancipation and Equal Rights

THE NORTON ESSAYS IN AMERICAN HISTORY
Under the general editorship of
HAROLD M. HYMAN

William P. Hobby Professor of American History
Rice University

EISENHOWER AND BERLIN, 1945: THE DECISION
TO HALT AT THE ELBE   *Stephen E. Ambrose*

THE MONEY QUESTION DURING RECONSTRUCTION
Walter T. K. Nugent

ANDREW JACKSON AND THE BANK WAR
Robert V. Remini

THE GREAT BULL MARKET: WALL STREET IN THE 1920's
Robert Sobel

THE JACKSONIAN ECONOMY   *Peter Temin*

A NEW ENGLAND TOWN: THE FIRST HUNDRED YEARS
Kenneth A. Lockridge

DIPLOMACY FOR VICTORY: FDR AND UNCONDITIONAL
SURRENDER   *Raymond G. O'Connor*

THE ORIGINS OF AMERICAN INTERVENTION IN THE
FIRST WORLD WAR   *Ross Gregory*

THE IMPEACHMENT AND TRIAL OF ANDREW JOHNSON
Michael Les Benedict

THE GENET MISSION   *Harry Ammon*

THE POLITICS OF NORMALCY: GOVERNMENTAL
THEORY AND PRACTCE IN THE HARDING–COOLIDGE ERA
Robert K. Murray

THE FAILURE OF THE NRA   *Bernard Bellush*

A HISTORY OF THE ICC   *Ari and Olive Hoogenboom*

BLACK IMAGES OF AMERICA   *Leonard Sweet*

DELIVER US FROM EVIL: AN INTERPRETATION OF
AMERICAN PROHIBITION   *Norman Clark*

A RESPECTABLE MINORITY: THE DEMOCRATIC PARTY
IN THE CIVIL WAR ERA, 1860–1868   *Joel H. Silbey*

EMANCIPATION AND EQUAL RIGHTS: POLITICS AND
CONSTITUTIONALISM IN THE CIVIL WAR ERA
Herman Belz

Emancipation and Equal Rights

*Politics and Constitutionalism
in the Civil War Era*

Herman Belz

W · W · NORTON & COMPANY · *New York · London*

Library of Congress Cataloging in Publication Data

Belz, Herman.
  Emancipation and equal rights.

  (The Norton essays in American history)
  Bibliography: p.
  Includes index.
  1. Reconstruction.   2. Afro-Americans—
History—1863–1877.   I. Title.
E668.B45   1978   973.8   78–16811
ISBN 0–393–05692–9
ISBN 0–393–09016–7 pbk.

1 2 3 4 5 6 7 8 9 0

1-22-79

For Arthur Bestor,
scholar and constitutionalist

Contents

Preface

THE INTENSE racial and social conflict that racked American society a decade ago caused a curious re-evaluation of slave emancipation and the constitutional decision for equal rights, which a century earlier had laid the foundation for modern advances in the sphere of civil rights. If it was necessary for black Americans to go so far as to engage in virtually revolutionary activity in order to achieve equality, many historians reasoned, then the release from bondage that occurred during the Civil War and the steps toward equality before the law taken during Reconstruction must have been regrettably, nay, tragically insubstantial. I am inclined to disagree with this judgment, not because I think that revolutionary or reformist action —a separate question in any case—was inappropriate in the circumstances that prevailed ten years ago, but because it presents an unhistorical view of past actions and events. By that I mean that it considers them principally in relation to present day concerns rather than in the context of their own time. Without denying the often very direct connection between past events and present tendencies in politics and society, I have tried in this book to present an accurate rendering of the events and ideas that in a political and constitutional sense marked the beginning of modern efforts to achieve racial integration on the basis of civil equality.

I acknowledge with pleasure and gratitude the valuable criticism and advice I have received in preparing this volume from George M. Dennison, trusted constitutional critic and friend, of Colorado State University, and from my colleagues Fred Nicklason, Ira Berlin, and George Callcott of the University of Maryland. The Graduate School of the University of Maryland,

and especially Dean David S. Sparks, assisted by providing a stipend to cover the cost of typing the manuscript. I owe a large debt of gratitude also to Professor Harold M. Hyman of Rice University for his cordial and steady encouragement, not only in the writing of this book but also in respect of other matters historical and professional.

HERMAN BELZ

Silver Spring, Maryland
March 1978

Introduction

THE SECTIONAL controversy that issued in the Civil War involved not only the morality of slavery but also and more fundamentally the nature of American political and social institutions. In comparative perspective American society was liberal and democratic from its very inception. Nevertheless it tolerated if it did not positively encourage an institution that, irrespective of the intentions of particular individuals, stood as a continual reproach to and contradiction of the democratic values that a growing portion of the American people regarded as the very basis of American nationality. The ability of slaves to carve out spheres of personal autonomy notwithstanding, slavery denied the right of four million black persons to the most elementary kind of self-determination. It literally denied the right of self-government that was the touchstone of the American polity. By 1861 moreover efforts to protect and promote slavery threatened the very integrity of the federal republic, eventually provoking northerners to fight in its defense. Once war began, the desire to preserve the Union merged with hostility toward slavery as the antithesis of republican institutions to produce the decision for emancipation. Amidst the profound social upheaval that the abolition of slavery caused, a combination of principled and expedient considerations led the Union Congress to pass a series of civil rights laws and constitutional amendments—the first in United States history—that insisted on national application of the principle of equality before the law in each state irrespective of race.

The principle of equal rights was a cardinal feature of the republican ideology that had sustained the American people in their revolutionary origins and guided them as they expanded territorially and politically in the nineteenth century. In the crisis of national life that marked the 1860s the equal rights idea provided a standard of value and a guideline for political action as Americans entered upon the uncharted social and civil landscape created by emancipation. Again considering matters in comparative perspective, one notes that civil and legal equality had come relatively easily for white male Americans in the eighteenth and nineteenth centuries. In part this was because Americans used the ideals of republican self-government and equal citizenship to define their national identity, rather than language, religion, history, or tradition which formed the bases of European nationalism. Given the broadly democratic character of American society, the logic of this highly rational and ideological political culture was toward the inclusion of all persons as citizens. Although in some states Negroes might become state, and therefore national citizens, in general they were the exception that proved the tendency or rule of democratic inclusiveness, especially in the antebellum period of heightened racial restrictiveness.

After abolishing slavery, however, in a radical reversal of outlook and policy, Americans took steps to include blacks in this ideological and institutional system. From the Dred Scott decision, which on the eve of the war declared them neither citizen nor alien but rather a kind of subject national without any rights, Negroes became American citizens with constitutionally protected privileges and immunities. Viewed in broad historical perspective, this abrupt change from exclusion to integration may appear to have been the inexorable result of the inner logic of the political culture. In a society that knows no gradations of citizenship the status of freedom necessarily carries with it equality of citizenship. Yet though freedom and equality may have described the tendency of American institutions—or more precisely, in view of the challenge presented by slavery, *a* tendency of American institutions—there was nothing inevitable about the civil rights laws and constitutional amendments adopted by Republican lawmakers in the 1860s. This fact becomes obvious when one considers the very different and decidedly anti-equalitarian proposals for racial policy offered by the Democratic party at the same time.

In short, Americans had choices as they wrestled with the problem of slavery and the results which followed its abolition, and the choices they made went far toward establishing integration and equal rights as the norm in American public life. It is of course necessary to point out that while Americans had reason to assert equality as a norm, other factors, including racial prejudice, kept them from making it a social reality in any comprehensive way. Yet the failure fully to realize the ideal of equality, lamentable though it was, should not obscure the greatly broadened scope of civil, political, and social activities that Negroes could and did in fact pursue as American citizens after emancipation. As a legal-constitutional structure the new civil rights dispensation did not by itself assure equalitarian results, but the success blacks enjoyed in vindicating their civil liberty would not have been possible without it. When one considers finally the gains blacks have made in the civil rights revolution of the past two decades, the importance of the original equal rights settlement of the slavery question stands out all the more clearly.

The idea of civil equality pointed the direction of post-emancipation public law within a system of assumptions, institutions, and rules about government that formed a second major component of American ideology. This system of beliefs and practices was constitutionalism, and it shaped and gave a distinct character to the political events surrounding emancipation.

Constitutionalism is an approach to the conduct of politics which rests on the assumption that the purpose of a constitution —in the United States a written constitution that is the proximate source of governing authority—is to restrict the power of government in the interest of individual liberty and self-determination. Still an important influence in American politics, the significance of constitutionalism was even more considerable in the Civil War era. Concern for preserving constitutional principle had been a central motive in the American Revolution, and after 1787 it led to swift acceptance and even veneration of the new federal Constitution. In an extensive, heterogeneous, and rapidly changing society constitutional principles were a source of national identity and stability. Problems of national unification, moreover, essentially constitutional in nature, were among the most important of the nineteenth century in the United States no less than in Europe. In the United States national growth occurred through the formation of new states in the western territories, a process that reinforced the habit of constitution-making that began during the Revolution. It is probably true also that because of the prevalent philosophical idealism of the age, which attributed causal significance to ideas in general, the nineteenth century mind took constitutional principles and issues more seriously than the more realist mind of the twentieth century, which tends to see material or economic forces as the chief motivating influence in political life.

Two substantive issues were of preeminent importance in the constitutionalism of the Civil War era. Federalism, the first of these issues, was rooted in the development of the American colonies in the seventeenth and eighteenth centuries as virtually autonomous parts of the British empire. A form of political organization, federalism divided power between local governments and a general or central government, yet provided that both kinds of governing authority share the same territory and population base. Several distinct approaches to federalism appeared in the nineteenth century. Chief Justice John Marshall, though recognizing state powers, expounded a theory of national-supremacy federalism which held that federal power properly exercised could in case of conflict supersede state power and control any person in American territory. Marshall's successor, Jacksonian Democrat Roger B. Taney, endorsed dual federalism, according to which the states and the federal government, neither of them supreme in any comprehensive or plenary sense, operated in mutually exclusive and reciprocally limiting spheres of power. Although dual federalism in theory placed the federal government and the states on an equal plane, in practice it emphasized strict construction of national powers and encouraged an expansion of state powers. Pro-slavery constitutional theorists such as John C. Calhoun offered yet another version of federalism that regarded the Union as a compact of states that retained unitary and indivisible sovereignty, while delegating a nondiscretionary, ministerial power to the federal government as their agent.

The Republican party that came to power in 1861 confounded these traditions of constitutional theory by blending national-supremacy federalism with recognition of the vitality and importance of the states to form what has aptly been called state-rights nationalism.[1] Repudiating state sovereignty, Lincoln's party in the 1850s sought a national solution to the slavery question by upholding congressional power to keep the territories free. In the secession crisis Republicans used John Marshall's idea of federal supremacy to defend the life of the national government. Yet in other respects the party that defended the Union relied on states' rights. In controversies over fugitive slaves, for example, Republicans interposed state power to prevent the carrying out of national law and uphold the right of free states to protect their citizens against deprivation of liberty. Furthermore, though regarding slavery as a national problem, they argued less for the application than for the withdrawal of federal power in all matters pertaining to slavery.

Republican defense of the Union in 1861 expressed a strong feeling of nationalism but not a desire to centralize American government. Politically an amalgam of Whigs and Democrats, Republicans in a constitutional sense resembled the former in their emphasis on Unionism and the latter in their identification of the Union with local self-government. Republican state-rights nationalism was proof that states' rights was a preoccupation not only of the South but of the North as well because it gave people at the local level power to control their individual and collective affairs. Relative to antebellum times, wartime exigencies were to require a considerable degree of centralization, but Republican state-rights nationalism checked this tendency.

1. I use the term employed by Phillip S. Paludan in his illuminating essay, "John Norton Pomeroy, State Rights Nationalist," *American Journal of Legal History*, XII (July 1968), 275–93.

"Centralism is the convergence of all the rays of power into one central point," the ardent Unionist Francis Lieber observed, while "nationalization is the diffusion of the same life-blood through a system of arteries, throughout a body politic. . . ."[2] In state-rights nationalism the states were the arteries through which flowed the life-blood of American nationality—the ideas and practices of local self-government.[3]

The nature of republican government was the second issue of fundamental importance in the constitutionalism of the Civil War era. Whereas federalism involved the relationship between and among the various levels of government in the United States, republicanism concerned the proper relationship between government and individual citizen. In the eighteenth century republican government meant nonmonarchical government resting on popular consent and participation. In the nineteenth century the republican tradition flourished, and with the quickening of democratic spirit produced variations on the theme of representative government. Jeffersonian Republicans and Federalists, Jacksonian Democrats and Whigs, gave different emphases to the theory and practice of republicanism.

Sharp controversies arose among diverse proponents of the republican tradition, but no differences that proved irreconcilable. When events in the 1840s forced Americans to consider the significance of slavery for republican government, however, American politics began to assume a more hostile, divisive character. Southerners defined republican government as local autonomy and, pointing to the example of slave-holding states during the American Revolution, said it was compatible with slavery. Northerners insisted that free government resting on consent could not tolerate an institution that utterly denied con-

2. Quoted in David Donald, *et al.*, *The Great Republic: A History of the American People* (2 vols.; Lexington, Mass., 1977), II, 772.

3. See generally Yehoshua Arieli, *Individualism and Nationalism in American Ideology* (Baltimore, 1966), and Phillip S. Paludan, "The American Civil War Considered as a Crisis in Law and Order," *American Historical Review*, LXXVII (October 1972), 1013–34.

sent, and hence condemned slavery as a desecration of republican values.[4]

Theoretically separable, the constitutional problems of federalism and republican government were inextricably connected in the slavery controversy. Northerners in the 1850s believed that the defense of slavery, in measures such as the fugitive slave act, the Dred Scott decision, and the proposal for a federal slave code in the territories, threatened both republican liberty and the federal principle of local self-government. When Lincoln's election seemed to place in jeopardy the security of their society, southerners invoked the principle of state sovereignty and the time-honored republican tradition of local self-determination, as they saw it, to form a new confederation of states. When finally the Confederate states attacked Fort Sumter, northerners took up arms to defend not merely a nation state but a federal Union of republican states. Both federalism and republicanism were at issue in the Civil War.

The decision to abolish slavery carried in its train important consequences for both federalism and the meaning of republican government. In order to confirm emancipation, Republican lawmakers restricted the plenary power over personal liberty and civil rights that states had enjoyed in the antebellum period, and enlarged federal authority in this sphere. They further insisted that in order to reenter the Union the states must agree not only to support the Constitution but also to accept a new conception of republican government. Equality before states' laws irrespective of race provided the foundation for this new conception.

This book examines the interrelated elements of equal rights ideology and constitutionalism that influenced the political struggles surrounding emancipation and the definition of Negro status during the Civil War and Reconstruction. It focuses on these elements but not to the exclusion of the more familiar facts of racial

4. On the constitutional history of the idea of republican government, see William M. Wiecek, *The Guarantee Clause of the U.S. Constitution* (Ithaca, 1972).

prejudice and party ambition that also played an essential role and that frequently dominate accounts of this period. Indeed, it takes these facts for granted. It is concerned rather to show that an accurate understanding of emancipation and its consequences requires attention to the role of formal ideological and institutional structures in mediating and refracting social and political forces. The abolition of slavery, which never in history had occurred on so large a scale, stirred political passions and racial fears, and these passions and fears intersected with ideological and constitutional considerations to produce the unique events that marked the introduction of equal citizenship into American public law.

Emancipation and Equal Rights

1

The Republican
Constitutional Imperative

ROOTED IN CONFLICTING conceptions of the federal
Union almost as old as the government itself, the American
Civil War was a constitutional crisis of the most profound sort.
After secession disrupted the Union, the purpose of the war in
the most fundamental sense became the determination of how
American government would be constituted. The federal republic of 1787 might be restored, a consolidated, sovereign
national government might evolve, or, at the opposite extreme,
two systems of federated states might be created. The crisis
involved more than the question of political organization, however, because the force and violence of organized warfare mili-
tated against, if they did not inherently contradict, the conduct
of politics by the rules and principles of constitutionalism. The
Civil War tested not only America's unique system of federalism but also its distinctive method of constitutional politics.

The twofold constitutional crisis that occurred during the
Civil War had its origin in the controversy over slavery. The
first aspect of the crisis—the problem of continental political
organization—took shape in the 1840s when westward expansion required Americans to define anew the relationship
between slavery and the republic. Southerners, proposing the theory of state sovereignty, argued that the slave states had exclusive power to decide all questions of law and policy concerning
slavery in the territories. After events in Kansas during the
1850s taught southerners that popular sovereignty would not
support their interests, the South demanded outright federal

protection of slavery based on the state sovereignty idea. They
got the protection they sought in the Dred Scott decision, in
which the Supreme Court said the Constitution guaranteed a
right to take slave property into the territories. They got it again
two years later in Ableman v. Booth when the Court, in upholding the fugitive slave act of 1850, vindicated the slave states'
laws authorizing the recapture of escaped slaves over the free
states' rules of personal liberty and due process.[1] Southerners
also sought, but failed to receive, federal protection in the form
of a congressional slave code for the territories that would have
adopted state slave codes as United States law.

Content to remain in the Union under these conditions,
southerners hoped that policies based on the principle of state
sovereignty would continue to protect their vital interests.
Whether a thoroughgoing application of that theory would have
brought about a substantive change in the nature of the Union,
by drastically curtailing both federal and free states' legislative
powers, it is perhaps impossible to say. At the least, events of
the 1850s indicated a tendency toward that result. This became
all the more clear in constitutional changes that slave state representatives proposed after South Carolina seceded in December
1860. At that time Robert Toombs of Georgia introduced
amendments that would have protected slave property in the
territories, guaranteed slavery protection from the U.S. government wherever its jurisdiction extended, imposed slave state
criminal laws on all states in matters pertaining to alleged fugitive slaves, required enforcement of the fugitive slave act of
1850 without writs of habeas corpus and trial by jury, and
insisted on congressional laws punishing invasion, insurrection,
or disturbing the domestic tranquility of any state. The better
known Crittenden compromise resolutions reiterated these slave
state demands and further proposed to prohibit the federal

1. Arthur Bestor, "State Sovereignty and Slavery: A Reinterpretation of Proslavery Constitutional Doctrine, 1846–1860," *Journal of the
Illinois State Historical Society*, LIV (Summer, 1961), 117–80, esp.
136–42, 162–72.

government from interfering with the slave trade between the territories and slave states. By irrepealable, unamendable constitutional amendments southerners thus tried permanently to alter the basic terms of federal-state political organization. Even southern moderates, as they contemplated reorganization or reconstruction of the Union in the secession winter, insisted on independence based on state sovereignty.[2]

The slavery controversy not only threatened the structure of federalism, it also challenged the rule of law, the second aspect of the consitutional crisis that the Civil War produced. Although imperfect in the manner of all institutions, slavery as an ideal type gave the master the right to make others an extension of his own personal will. It thus contradicted the fundamental principle of republican government and American political institutions, the notion of consent. Nor was the negation merely theoretical or confined to the private sphere of the household. In political struggles in the 1850s proslavery forces took actions that northerners regarded as lawless and coercive. Congressional gag rules, the mobbing of abolitionist speakers, interference with the mails and denial of free speech in the South, fugitive slave recaptures which abrogated free states' due process of law, the reliance on fraud and violence in the attempt to establish slavery in Kansas, the caning of Massachusetts Senator Charles Sumner in the Senate chamber—all were taken as evidence of the lawlessness of the slave power.[3]

As secession brought to a climax the southern challenge to traditional federalism, so too it signified a profound escalation

2. John W. Burgess, *The Civil War and the Constitution, 1859–1865* (2 vols.; New York, 1901), I, 96–98; Harold M. Hyman, "Reconstruction and Political-Constitutional Institutions: The Popular Expression," in Hyman, ed., *New Frontiers of the American Reconstruction* (Urbana, 1966), 8–9; William S. Hitchcock, "Southern Moderates and Secession: Senator Robert M. T. Hunter's Call for Union," *Journal of American History*, LIX (March, 1973), 871–84.

3. Phillip S. Paludan, "Law and Equal Rights: The Civil War Encounter: A Study of Legal Minds in the Civil War Era," Ph.D. dissertation, University of Illinois, 1968, pp. 1–13.

of the slave interest's assault on the rule of law. Because northerners identified local self-government with the Union ordained by the Constitution, they regarded the attempt to destroy the Union as a threat to constitutional government. Agreeing with Lincoln that the logic of secession was anarchistic, they concluded after the attack on Fort Sumter that force must not be allowed to supersede the peaceful methods of constitutionalism. Underlying this outlook was the fact that the political ideal of local self-government under law was a stabilizing, unifying force in the decentralized, heterogeneous, and rapidly changing society of mid-nineteenth-century America. Indeed local self-government was perhaps the chief basis of American nationality. To uphold and extend this constitutional imperative, as well as to preserve the political organization of federal Union, northerners went to war.[4]

In the situation that existed in April 1861 these broader concerns presented themselves in the form of a simpler, more immediate issue. "The question now is not one of Union," wrote an antislavery correspondent, "*but of power*. Shall the Montgomery [i.e. Confederate] government be the leading, prevailing power on this continent, or shall the old United States government still retain its supremacy?"[5] President Lincoln swiftly provided an answer. Calling up 75,000 state militia, proclaiming a blockade of southern ports, increasing the size of the army and ordering money to be spent from the Treasury without congressional authorization, and instituting martial law by suspending the privilege of the writ of habeas corpus which protected individuals against illegal and arbitrary detention, Lincoln in a few weeks created a crisis government.

Many believed at the time that Lincoln's actions were patently unconstitutional. The most resounding assertion of this

4. Phillip S. Paludan, "The American Civil War Considered as a Crisis in Law and Order," *American Historical Review*, LXXVII (October, 1972), 1013–34; Yehoshua Arieli, *Individualism and Nationalism in American Ideology* (Baltimore, 1966).

5. *National Anti-Slavery Standard*, April 20, 1861.

view came at the very beginning of the war when Chief Justice Roger B. Taney, in the case of Ex parte Merryman in the federal circuit court in Maryland, held that only Congress could suspend the privilege of the writ of habeas corpus and that persons arrested under Lincoln's suspension order were wrongly detained. Most contemporaries disagreed, and the judgment of history has been otherwise. To some extent the historian William A. Dunning reflected Taney's critical evaluation in stating that the President's acts revolutionized the practice of the government and undermined the long standing belief that even in preserving its authority the government must respect constitutional limitations. Lincoln substituted popular demand for legal mandate, Dunning wrote, and the idea of a government restricted by the written organic law began to grow dim. Nevertheless, realist that he was, Dunning concluded that Lincoln's temporary dictatorship represented an adaptation to unprecedented events and illustrated a new principle in the constitutional system. Lincoln's emergency rule, in other words, was a constitutional dictatorship.[6]

Viewing Lincoln's emergency measures in this way, as most northerners did, led to the corollary judgment that the Constitution provided an adequate basis for dealing with the exigencies of war. While in retrospect the eventual triumph of the Union and the vindication of the Constitution may cause this perception of adequacy to seem unremarkable, in actuality it was not, for the tribulations of the secession winter had inspired keen apprehension about the ability of existing laws and institutions to withstand the crisis. Among some Unionists, including congressional leader Thaddeus Stevens, this outlook led to

6. William A. Dunning, *Essays on the Civil War and Reconstruction* (New York: Harper Torchbook, 1965), 15–23; Clinton Rossiter, *Constitutional Dictatorship: Crisis Government in the Modern Democracies* (Princeton, 1948), Ch. XV; Andrew C. McLaughlin, "Lincoln, the Constitution, and Democracy," *International Journal of Ethics*, XLVII (October 1936), 1–24; James G. Randall, *Lincoln the Liberal Statesman* (New York, 1947), 118–34.

the conclusion that the war simply abrogated the Constitution in all matters concerning the suppression of rebellion.[7] The vast majority of Republicans, however, though in accordance with the view of the founding fathers recognizing war as profoundly different from peace, thought it could and must be dealt with within the existing legal framework.[8] It was significant therefore that the Civil War did not produce anything like a *kriegzustand*, or arbitrary, extra-constitutional, indefinitely prolonged condition of emergency rule.[9]

The most obvious practical import of the doctrine of constitutional adequacy was the belief that legitimate power existed for suppressing the rebellion and meeting the internal security needs of the government. One specific source of power was the guarantee clause of the Constitution, which states that the United states shall guarantee to each state in the Union a republican form of government. In explaining why secession must be resisted, for example, Lincoln in his special message to Congress in July 1861 said it was for the purpose of upholding the constitutional guarantee that each state have a republican government.[10] Yet because the guarantee clause seemed more concerned with nonmilitary questions about the nature of politi-

7. James Albert Woodburn, "The Attitude of Thaddeus Stevens Toward the Conduct of the Civil War," *American Historical Association Annual Report*, 1906 (2 vols.; Washington, 1908), I, 213–31; *Congressional Globe*, 37 Cong., 1 Sess., 414 (August 2, 1861), remarks of Thaddeus Stevens.

8. Alfred H. Kelly, "The Constitution and the War Power: Some Observations," paper presented before the Foreign Relations Committee, U.S. Senate, March 9, 1971, p. 2. Kelly points out that in early modern history war and peace were not clearly separated, war being seen as the normal business of states. The framers of the American constitution, in contrast, tried to separate war and peace by treating the former as extraordinary and hence requiring special considerations and procedures before it could be undertaken.

9. James G. Randall, *Constitutional Problems Under Lincoln*, rev. ed. (Urbana, 1951), 25–26; Harold M. Hyman, *A More Perfect Union: The Impact of the Civil War and Reconstruction on the Constitution* (New York, 1973), 81–140.

10. William M. Wieck, *The Guarantee Clause of the U.S. Constitution* (Ithaca, 1972), 170–71; Roy P. Basler et al., eds., *The Collected Works of Abraham Lincoln* (9 vols.; New Brunswick, 1953–55), IV, 440.

cal institutions, it was more appropriate for reconstruction than for wartime military purposes.

A more relevant source of wartime power within the framework of the belief in constitutional adequacy was the doctrine of martial law. During the Civil War the Union government enjoyed the use of a theory of martial law that only recently had been significantly broadened in its scope and effect. In the early national period martial law, referring to the terms and conditions under which military power might govern civilians, had received a narrow construction. Only for defensive purposes, in the event of actual invasion or in time of war, could military power control civil affairs. In the 1840s, however, under the pressure of domestic political agitation and foreign war, a broader definition of martial law evolved. The new view allowed government officials at their discretion to suspend civil law and use military power to govern society and preserve existing authority, even as in a state of actual warfare.[11]

In 1862 legal commentator Timothy Farrar employed this broadened conception in writing that martial law, defined simply as the rights of war, was paramount to all other law whenever the public safety demanded it. With this conclusion in mind Farrar asserted that the Constitution was fully adequate to the exigencies of government in wartime and to the preservation of the Union.[12] In similar fashion William Whiting, Solicitor in the War Department, offered a sweeping view of federal power that rested on the new teaching about martial law. Whiting held that the war authorized the government to suspend ordinary civil administration in rebel areas and to govern by martial law. Military government would not deprive persons of constitutional rights, he reasoned, "because *martial law*, when in force, is *constitutional* law." Nor was martial law confined to the immediate area of hostilities. It extended, Whiting wrote, any-

11. George M. Dennison, "Martial Law: The Development of a Theory of Emergency Powers, 1776–1861," *American Journal of Legal History*, XVIII (January 1974), 52–79.

12. Timothy Farrar, "The Adequacy of the Constitution," *New Englander*, XXI (January 1862), 52, 63.

where help was given to the enemy. Advancing such capacious doctrines of power, Whiting received praise for what one radical journal called the "*solvitur ambulando,* or 'Jump up and try,' method [of constitutional interpretation] which is swiftly transforming the compromises of the Constitution into statutes of Freedom."[13]

Whiting denied that martial law was mere force or necessity.[14] Nevertheless, throughout his widely circulated treatise on war powers, he emphasized the necessity for vigor and energy in government and devoted little attention to constitutional restraints. If Whiting did not quite equate necessity with the supreme law, he tended in that direction. In contrast other Republicans thought the doctrine of constitutional adequacy required clearer recognition of the continued need for limitations on government power. A reviewer of Whiting's war powers tract wrote, for example, that while almost all Unionists believed the government could legitimately exercise sovereign and belligerent rights against the rebels, they also stressed the need to subject the government to certain restrictions. Yet Whiting's concern for virtually unlimited power ignored this consideration.[15]

Early in the war Henry Winter Davis of Maryland, a leading Republican representative in the Thirty-eighth Congress, asserted a theory of constitutional adequacy that laid stress on limiting as well as galvanizing governmental power. By the end of the Buchanan administration, Davis observed, the weakening of the constitutional structure required an infusion of power. Lincoln's crisis government supplied this want, but it also raised questions about the rule of law. Citing General Frémont's order of martial law and military emancipation in Missouri, Davis in October 1861 warned that excessive reliance on military power

13. William Whiting, *War Powers Under the Constitution of the United States,* 43rd ed. (Boston, 1871), 64, 201–2; Boston *Commonwealth,* August 21, 1863.

14. Whiting, *War Powers,* 267.

15. Anon., "Prerogative Rights and Public Law," *Monthly Law Reporter,* XXV (January 1863), 130, 136.

was potentially revolutionary. Suspension of the writ of habeas corpus, the closing down of opposition newspapers, and the use of martial law in places where civil institutions existed signified to Davis a desire to rely on the doctrine of necessity, and a corresponding doubt about the adequacy of the Constitution to meet the needs of war. Correctly understood, Davis reasoned, the sufficiency of the Constitution meant that those in power must be held responsible not just for energy but for legality and constitutionality as well. Otherwise executive discretion and military force would become the approved basis of government action, and "We pass from the constitutional freedom of America to the democratic despotism of France." Then, exclaimed Davis, necessity and expediency would be the supreme law, the President its supreme interpreter, and his perception of what the people would allow the only restriction on government action. To guard against any such development and preserve American republicanism, Davis urged "rigid adherence to written law, to the will of the people proclaimed in constitutional forms."[16]

Davis of course had political reasons for criticizing executive power and military rule. As a border state man he keenly understood the destructive impact that war and military occupation could have, and as yet he did not favor abolition. His political views therefore complemented and influenced his constitutional outlook. But this of course is the way that constitutional principles and rules are supposed to function, in the pursuance of substantive political objectives. What is significant is that often during the Civil War Republican lawmakers who agreed with the political aims of the Lincoln administration, such as Davis in 1861, nevertheless raised constitutional objections to government actions.

Senator Lyman Trumbull of Illinois emerged as the foremost Republican critic of executive power in the Thirty-seventh Congress. Like Davis, Trumbull's chief argument was that the Constitution—limitations and all—provided an adequate basis

16. Henry Winter Davis, *Speeches and Addresses* (New York, 1867), 260–62, 265, 271, 281–91.

for fighting the war. Denying the adage *inter arma silent leges* (laws are silent during war), he believed Congress had the responsibility to suppress the rebellion in a constitutional and legal manner.[17] Trumbull placed special importance on protecting citizens' liberties. Where courts were overborne the army could properly regulate civil affairs, he reasoned, but to arrest persons in places not in the theater of war was arbitrary and despotic. Rejecting the appeal to necessity and the public safety, which theorists such as Whiting entertained approvingly,[18] Trumbull asked: "Has the Constitution no meaning, and are laws to have no effect?"[19]

At the special session of Congress in July 1861, Trumbull introduced a far-reaching bill for the regulation of military power in rebellious territory that expressed the theory of constitutional adequacy. Intended to establish the principle of civilian control of the military, the measure empowered Union commanders to make local police regulations for the purpose of suppressing rebellion, restoring order, and protecting the lives and property of inhabitants.[20] Several Republicans objected to the measure on the ground that under the laws of war the President could exercise the powers in question independently of Congress.[21] A larger number of administration supporters, however, preferred to see Congress regulate executive control of occupied rebel districts. Especially noteworthy were the arguments of conservative Republicans John C. Ten Eyck, Ira Harris, and Orville H. Browning that the regulation of civil affairs should not be left to the discretion of the military.[22] Although the bill was too controversial in nature for Congress to deal with at this time, its consideration foreshadowed subsequent efforts to

17. *Cong. Globe*, 37 Cong., 1 Sess., 337 (July 30, 1861).
18. Whiting, *War Powers*, 52, 268.
19. *Cong. Globe*, 37 Cong., 2 Sess., 91 (December 16, 1861).
20. 37th Congress, S. No. 33, July 17, 1861, file of printed bills of the U.S. Congress, Library of Congress.
21. *Cong. Globe*, 37 Cong., 1 Sess., 340 (July 30, 1861), remarks of Edgar Cowan, 374 (August 1, 1861), remarks of Jacob Collamer.
22. Ibid., 342 (July 30, 1861), remarks of John Ten Eyck, 372 (August 1, 1861), remarks of Orville Browning and Ira Harris.

regulate executive control of the military and identified an important element in the Republican constitutional imperative.

The creation of the Joint Committee on the Conduct of the War in December 1861 further expressed Republican lawmakers' intention to restrain executive power and to affirm civilian control of the military. Although radicals later tried to dominate this committee, its formation did not rest on anti-Lincoln sentiments. Rather it grew out of frustration with military failure, resentment against the West Point professional officer class, and a desire to promote emancipation for military purposes. Constitutionally the committee has been criticized for interfering with executive management of military operations and for not attending to the proper legislative role of making rules for the conduct of the war.[23] The dramatic ascendancy of the executive in the first year of the war, however, and the unprecedented nature of the crisis in which political and military issues became inextricably connected, make it difficult to agree with this judgment.

Insofar as the joint committee interfered with strictly military decisions and employed unfair methods of investigation, it may be faulted on constitutional grounds. On the other hand the committee upheld the constitutional principle of civilian control of the military. Legislative investigations of military campaigns were a long established part of governmental practice, and Republican lawmakers firmly believed, in the words of William Pitt Fessenden of Maine, that Congress had a duty "to keep an anxious, watchful eye over all the executive agents who are carrying on the war. . . ."[24] Under the circumstances, moreover, the whole subject of war powers lacked precise definition, which meant that the limits of executive and legislative roles had to be drawn. With no clear model to follow, the Joint Committee on the Conduct of the War helped give a congressional cast to the system of crisis government that the war produced. Finally, though often acting as a pressure group for

23. Alfred H. Kelly and Winfred A. Harbison, *The American Constitution: Its Origin and Development*, 4th ed. (New York, 1970), 428.
24. *Cong. Globe*, 37 Cong., 2 Sess., 31 (December 9, 1861).

emancipationist opinion and as a kind of war council, the joint committee on balance facilitated executive-legislative coopera- tion and frequently became a useful instrument of presidential purpose.[25]

Congress further vindicated the principle of legislative con- trol of executive power in the Habeas Corpus Act of 1863. From the start of the war the President had in certain places suspended the writ of habeas corpus and organized an internal security program. The legal question these actions prompted was whether the President possessed constitutional authority to take them, or whether they required legislative authorization. Conservative Republicans, denying any congressional authority in the matter, looked upon the administration's anti-disloyalty policy as constitutional.[26] The majority of Republican law- makers, however, though unwilling to say that the President had acted illegally in suspending the writ, favored legislation that would unquestionably legitimize past executive action and as- sert congressional power over the subject. Accordingly the act of March 1863 stated that the President "is authorized" during the existing rebellion to suspend the writ of habeas corpus. This proposition compromised the legal question by leaving it un- clear whether the authorization came from Congress or the Constitution. More important, the act required the secretaries of State and War to furnish lists of political prisoners to federal courts for grand jury indictment or release, and required offi- cers in charge of prisoners to obey court orders. Congress thus

25. Hans L. Trefousse, "The Joint Committee on the Conduct of the War: A Reassessment," *Civil War History*, X (March 1964), 5–19; W. W. Pierson, Jr., "The Committee on the Conduct of the Civil War," *American Historical Review*, XXIII (April 1918), 550–76; T. Harry Williams, "The Committee on the Conduct of the War: An Experiment in Civilian Control," *Journal of the American Military Institute*, III (Fall, 1939), 139–56; Marcus Cunliffe, *Soldiers and Civilians: The Martial Spirit in America 1775–1865* (Boston, 1968), 318–334; Rossiter, *Constitutional Dictatorship*, 232.

26. *Cong. Globe*, 37 Cong., 2 Sess., 157 (December 22, 1862), re- marks of Henry S. Lane.

confirmed previous court action but successfully placed restrictions on further executive use of military power.[27]

More so than in matters of internal security and the conduct of the war, Republican lawmakers tried to regulate and restrict executive authority over reconstruction. To be sure, as military occupation of insurgent territory evolved into the first stage of reorganizing loyal state governments, the executive had a role to play in reconstruction. In the spring of 1862 Lincoln gave evidence of this fact in appointing military governors in four seceded states and in encouraging the election of members of Congress. Nevertheless, since the essence of reconstruction concerned reorganization of civil authority and revision of state constitutions and laws, sound reasons existed for regarding it as preeminently legislative in character. This assumption formed the basis for the numerous reconstruction plans that Republicans introduced into the Thirty-seventh and Thirty-eighth Congresses. While these plans did not deny an important role to the executive, they did propose formal legal limitations on executive discretion in reconstruction.

Throughout 1862 doubts about the legal authority of Lincoln's military governors and objections to the irregularity of administration policy in this sphere became more pronounced. In July a Republican correspondent, expressing the growing dissatisfaction, argued that the necessity for some law governing reconstruction was daily becoming more apparent.[28] Congressional Republicans meanwhile came to see the issue, in the words of Senator Ira Harris of New York, as "whether or not the President shall go on appointing Governors for the rebel States, as we get possession of them, without any authority, perhaps, of law, as a mere matter of necessity, or whether we shall regulate it by act of Congress."[29] When in December

27. Hyman, *A More Perfect Union*, 249–53; George Clarke Sellery, *Lincoln's Suspension of Habeas Corpus as Viewed by Congress*, Bulletin of the University of Wisconsin, No. 149 (April, 1907), pp. 213–86.
28. Cincinnati *Daily Gazette*, July 12, 1862.
29. *Cong. Globe*, 37 Cong., 3 Sess., 1507 (March 3, 1863).

1863 Lincoln sought to make presidential policy more systematic by issuing his amnesty and reconstruction proclamation, Republican lawmakers accepted the substance of his policy but questioned it on constitutional grounds. "The most trembling conservative in Congress," observed an antislavery correspondent in January 1864, "is compelled to admit that *some* legislation is necessary to revive the old State organizations."[30]

Passage of the Wade-Davis bill in July 1864 depended heavily on the belief that reconstruction required deliberation and action through legislation, rather than simply administration policy effected by proclamations.[31] Reflecting congressional sentiment, the Cincinnati *Gazette* asserted that "reconstruction should be brought forth in its own natural time, founded on the supreme law of the land . . . and on the support of the loyal inhabitants."[32] Based on the constitutional guarantee of republican government to each state in the Union, which at the very least seemed to preclude military government,[33] the Wade-Davis plan proposed to supervise state reorganization by formal procedures of law.[34] It thus rejected the administration's expansive conception of martial law as inappropriate for forming civil institutions.

Congressional regulation of executive power not only expressed the theory of constitutional adequacy, it also rested upon the principle of the separation of powers. Although Civil War Republican lawmakers have often been seen as advocating congressional hegemony in contradiction of this principle, their actions vis-à-vis the executive are best understood as an attempt to implement the separation of powers doctrine in accordance with its historic purpose.

The separation of powers evolved in seventeenth century England as a means by which parliamentary forces limited the

30. *National Anti-Slavery Standard*, January 30, 1864.
31. Cincinnati *Daily Commercial*, February 4, 1864.
32. Cincinnati *Daily Gazette*, April 29, 1864.
33. Wiecek, *The Guarantee Clause of the U.S. Constitution*, 173.
34. Anon., "The Legal Status of the Rebel States Before and After Their Conquest," *Monthly Law Reporter*, XXVI (August 1864), 551–54.

royal authority to executive and administrative functions and acquired for themselves the power to make law. It was, in other words, a revolutionary instrument that the rising bourgeoisie used in the struggle for sovereignty that dominated English political life throughout the century. Assimilated into the classical balanced constitution of the eighteenth century, the separation of powers became in America the basic organizing principle of revolutionary constitutionalism when the American colonies achieved independence.[35]

Rejecting the mixed government of the colonial period, in which the elected assembly shared legislative power with governor and council, Americans founded republican governments that gave law-making power to the people's representatives and reduced the governor to merely executive duties. In the 1780s, when it appeared that state legislatures were gaining too much power and were usurping executive and judicial functions, a reaction against radical or extreme application of the separation of powers doctrine set in. The result was a movement for constitutional reform, culminating in the Federal Convention of 1787, which modified the pure theory of separation of powers by reintroducing a limited sharing of powers (called checks and balances) derived from the theory of mixed government. Separation of powers *and* checks and balances, as seen, for example, in the assignment of the law-making power to Congress with limited participation by the President through a veto, thus became a fundamental tenet of American constitutionalism. Yet the pure or radical theory of the separation of powers did not cease to be relevant. On the contrary, it continued to have wide appeal and remained available as an instrument of constitutional politics.[36]

Considered in the light of this historic pattern, Republican assertions of legislative power during the Civil War were intended to implement the pure doctrine of the separation of powers. It was this purpose that ultimately justified congres-

35. Cf. M. J. C. Vile, *Constitutionalism and the Separation of Powers* (Oxford, 1967), 21–118.
36. Ibid., 119–175.

sional attempts to check executive power and to shape government policy in conducting the war, promoting emancipation, and supervising the process of reconstruction. When we note further that during the Civil War and Reconstruction the Republican party effected sweeping political, social, and economic changes by abolishing slavery and overthrowing the southern ruling class, we may view the separation of powers as a revolutionary constitutional instrument.

The confiscation debate of 1862 throws light on the content of separation of powers thinking in the Republican constitutional imperative. Although Republicans disagreed on whether property should be taken primarily for wartime or postwar reconstruction purposes, almost all of them endorsed confiscation.[37] The sharpest controversy concerned the respective powers of President and Congress in the matter. Opponents of confiscation legislation held that under the laws of war the executive could take enemy property without congressional authorization. In fact, argued conservative Republicans such as Orville H. Browning of Illinois, confiscation by act of Congress would usurp the war power of the President.[38] Most Republicans, however, apprehensive about executive ascendancy despite their personal confidence in Lincoln, appealed to the pure separation of powers theory in supporting a confiscation law.

The basic argument was that as the objects and duration of the war were proper subjects of legislation, and as Congress under the separation of powers possessed the law-making power, so Congress could pass a confiscation act affecting in a broad way the conduct of the war. The President was commander-in-chief, observed Senator Jacob Howard in support of confiscation measures, but this did not place him above laws passed by Congress in pursuance of its war-related powers.

37. John Syrett, "The Confiscation Acts: Efforts at Reconstruction during the Civil War," Ph.D. dissertation, University of Wisconsin, 1971.
38. *Cong. Globe*, 37 Cong., 2 Sess., 1136 (March 10, 1862), 1857 (April 29, 1862), 2918–20 (June 25, 1862), remarks of Orville Browning, 1879–80 (April 30, 1862), remarks of Edgar Cowan, 1922 (May 2, 1862), remarks of Jacob Collamer.

John Sherman similarly contended that the President could conduct the war "only in the manner and in the mode we may prescribe by law," while Benjamin F. Wade, reminding his colleagues that they formed "the legislative power," insisted it was for Congress to lay down the rules and principles that the executive must follow in commanding the military. Invoking the pure separation of powers doctrine, Wade reasoned that the President could not make law or formulate rules outside his strictly military jurisdiction.[39]

Reliance on classic separation of powers theory led to a denial of discretionary authority on the part of the executive. Arguing that the President must execute the law in time of war as well as peace, Lyman Trumbull equated executive discretion with unlimited presidential power and called it dangerous to republicanism. When conservative Republican Edgar Cowan defiantly said that even if Congress passed a confiscation law the President could choose to ignore it, John P. Hale rejected the notion as absurd. Why would Congress ever pass any act, Hale asked, if everything depended on the President? Henry Winter Davis summarized the fundamental tenet in the radical separation of powers doctrine: "The President, of himself, has no power to do any thing. He is the executor of the laws. . . . He has no discretion vested in him."[40]

Republicans strengthened their appeal to the separation of powers by linking it with the tradition of popular sovereignty. They thus offered as a counter force to the executive not simply a doctrine of power but a doctrine of popular power. Viewing confiscation as an incident of sovereignty, Alexander H. Rice of Massachusetts held that supreme authority resided ultimately in the people and immediately in their representatives in Congress. According to Wade, the founding fathers lodged supervisory

39. Ibid., 1718 (April 18, 1862), remarks of Jacob Howard, 1784 (April 23, 1862), 1917–18 (May 2, 1862), 2930 (June 25, 1862), remarks of Benjamin F. Wade.
40. Ibid., 2972 (June 27, 1862), remarks of Lyman Trumbull, 1881–82 (April 30, 1862), remarks of John P. Hale; Davis, *Speeches and Addresses*, 274.

control over executive officers in Congress, which in turn derived its power from the people at frequent intervals. Several members used the language of sovereignty to describe the role of Congress. "There is a supreme power in this Government," declared Hale of New Hampshire, which is conferred "upon the representatives of the great popular mass of the nation." Denying that the executive or judiciary enjoyed any share of the supreme power, Morton Wilkinson said the sovereignty of the nation lay "buried with the people" who exercised it through elected representatives. Jacob Howard put the matter succinctly in stating that the highest function of national sovereignty was the law-making power given to Congress. And if Congress allowed the President to control confiscation through the military power, Howard concluded, it would abdicate this sovereign power and permit executive decrees to become the law of the republic.[41]

Legislative regulation of the executive received further sanction from explicit constitutional provisions that in effect created a congressional war power. To begin with, the framers of the Constitution gave Congress the power to declare war, in order that the abnormal condition of war should be entered into only for reasons that the people clearly understood and approved.[42] Republican lawmakers naturally seized on this fact to strengthen their claim to determine government war policy. Congress possessing the power over war or peace, reasoned Jacob Howard, it "must necessarily move and, directly or indirectly, control all the instruments and operations of war."[43]

41. *Cong. Globe*, 37 Cong., 2 Sess., Appendix, 208 (May 26, 1862), remarks of Alexander H. Rice, 2928–29 (June 25, 1862), remarks of Benjamin F. Wade and John P. Hale, 2991–92 (June 28, 1862), remarks of Morton Wilkinson, 2968–69 (June 27, 1862), remarks of Jacob Howard.

42. Kelly, "The Constitution and the War Power"; Arthur Bestor, "Separation of Powers in the Domain of Foreign Affairs: The Intent of the Constitution Historically Examined," *Seton Hall Law Review*, V (Spring 1974), 597.

43. *Cong. Globe*, 37 Cong., 2 Sess., 2968 (June 27, 1862).

This did not mean that Congress had tactical, battlefield authority. To prevent legislative interference with the executive in that sphere the framers gave the law-making branch the power to "declare war," not to "make war."[44] Congress was, however, given the power to raise armies and navies, make laws for the government of military forces, provide for calling up the militia to execute the laws and suppress insurrection, and make rules concerning captures on land and water. All of these specific powers, in the opinion of Republican legislators, added up to a general war-making power that enabled Congress to concern itself with the principles and purposes of military action. Jacob Howard spoke for most of his colleagues when he said "it is idle to talk of a war-making power independent of the law-making power."[45]

The Republican outlook on congressional supervision of the executive and the separation of powers received clear expression from Sidney George Fisher in his well known constitutional treatise, *The Trial of the Constitution*, in 1862. Asserting that free government depended on the separation of powers, Fisher argued against concentration of power in any single department. To guard against this concentration and preserve liberty, he proposed that each branch be given a limited share in the power of the other two.[46] This did not mean, however, that Congress and the President were equal. On the contrary, Fisher reasoned, informed by public opinion Congress "originates, thinks, plans, and wills," whereas the executive merely applies the will of the legislature. As thought was superior to action, said Fisher, so the legislature was superior to the executive. Furthermore, viewing law as a command from a superior to an inferior that re-

44. Bestor, "Separation of Powers in the Domain of Foreign Affairs," 602–10.

45. *Cong. Globe*, 37 Cong., 2 Sess., 2968 (June 27, 1862).

46. Fisher thus proposed checks and balances in the traditional approach to separation of powers in America. He did not, as William H. Riker argued, seek to abolish the separation of powers. Cf. Riker, "Sidney George Fisher and the Separation of Powers During the Civil War," *Journal of the History of Ideas*, XV (June 1954), 397–412.

quired obedience, Fisher held that the law-making power implied superiority. Equating sovereignty with the law-making function, he concluded: "Given a free people and a representative Government, and the Legislature must be supreme."[47]

At this point a contradiction readily becomes apparent. Insisting on constitutional adequacy and limitations on government, Republicans also appealed to the supremacy of the law-making power. How, one is forced to ask, could Congress, the supreme law-making power, be kept from dominating the other parts of the government and violating the Constitution?

One approach to the problem was to deny that any inherent contradiction existed between the idea of limited government under a written constitution and legislative supremacy. Thus John P. Hale referred to Congress as "limited, created, measured and restrained by law," while Jacob Howard said the law-making power was bound by the supreme law of the Constitution. These assertions may be taken at a certain discount, however, for constitutional limitations had a way of yielding to legislative formulations based on the war power, which as we have seen was regarded as constitutional.[48] A more effective limitation on the law-making branch was the power of the President under the separation of powers and checks and balances system. Lincoln gave evidence of this power in July 1862 when he used the threat of a veto to get Congress to accept his view of confiscation as lasting only during the lifetime of the offender. He used the veto again on reconstruction, and in the cabinet crisis of December 1862 he employed consummate political skill to prevent a change in the administration that Republican senators demanded.

Beyond the means available to the President, however,

47. Sidney George Fisher, *The Trial of the Constitution* (Philadelphia, 1862), 46, 51, 54.

48. For example, Howard said that the constitutional requirement of jury trial could not be changed by Congress. He reasoned, however, that instead of relying on judicial power to effect confiscation, which would entail recognition of the right of jury trial, Congress could confiscate under the war power. *Cong. Globe*, 37 Cong., 2 Sess., Appendix, 305–7 (June 24, 1862).

which in actuality Lincoln used sparingly,[49] legislative supremacy was limited by popular sovereignty as embodied in electoral institutions. While in the modern age of media-dominated politics this method may seem ineffective, in the nineteenth century it was regarded as the most important single restraint on the law-making power. Chief Justice John Marshall explained the theory in 1824 when he said the wisdom and discretion of Congress, its identity with the people, and the influence its constituents possessed at elections, were the restraints on which the people must rely in all representative government.[50] Sidney George Fisher's wartime constitutional analysis underscored the same point. The legislature was supreme, Fisher wrote, "but so long as the people love liberty and reverence traditions and ancient rights, it cannot alter the Constitution against their will." The security of the people consisted in their control of Congress by the ballot box.[51] While Fisher's conclusion may seem merely theoretical, corroborating evidence suggests that legislative moderation among Republicans resulted from the need to appeal to broad constituencies in closely contested districts.[52] Among the effects that can be attributed to the continuance of party politics at the North, therefore, might be included limitation of the law-making power.[53]

Congressional assertions of law-making supremacy and attempts to regulate executive power were not, despite their political implications, primarily radical-inspired efforts designed to express dissatisfaction with the Lincoln administration. Supported by large numbers of moderate Republicans, they repre-

49. Cf. David Donald, "A Whig in the White House," in *Lincoln Reconsidered* (New York, 1961). Lincoln used his powers vigorously in matters pertaining to the conduct of the war, emancipation, and reconstruction, but in nonmilitary affairs he generally deferred to Congress.

50. Gibbons *v.* Ogden, 9 *Wheaton* 197 (1824).

51. Fisher, *Trial of the Constitution*, 41, 45.

52. Cf. David Donald, *The Politics of Reconstruction 1863–1867* (Baton Rouge, 1965).

53. Eric L. McKitrick, "Party Politics and the Union and Confederate War Efforts," in W. N. Chambers and W. D. Burnham, eds., *The American Party Systems: Stages of Political Development* (New York, 1967), 117–51.

sented an appeal to the idea of self-government through legislative supremacy, one of the fundamental elements in the American constitutional tradition.[54] The separation of powers, which gave law-making authority to the people's representatives, provided the specific means for implementing this long established notion. Along with insistence on the adequacy of the Constitution—a Constitution that included both powers and limitations—the separation principle lay at the heart of the Republican constitutional imperative.

While constitutional theories and ideas were by no means merely derivative of politics, they possessed undoubted political significance. Embodying basic values in the society, they were ultimately justified as instruments for the conduct of politics. It is to the substantive political issues that developed within the Republican constitutional framework that we now turn.

54. Cf. Willmoore Kendall and George W. Carey, *The Basic Symbols of the American Political Tradition* (Baton Rouge, 1970), 138–43.

2

Confiscation, Emancipation, and the Question of War Aims

THE ATTACK on Fort Sumter abruptly altered the focus of northern politics. Rather than the kind of union Americans desired, the overriding question became the survival of the Union itself. The earlier problem of the relationship of slavery to the Union did not cease to be pertinent, however, for no matter how much Republican leaders might profess the exclusive purpose of maintaining the Union, the possibility existed that military action to suppress the rebellion might result in widespread slave emancipation. Though the slavery issue might now be approached as means rather than end, its resolution remained the question of questions in American politics.

The slavery issue formed the basis not only for partisan alignment but also for factional division within the Republican party among radicals, moderates, and conservatives. The content of these distinctions of course changed over time. Before the war radicalism signified opposition to the spread of slavery and a commitment to its ultimate extinction. Once hostilities began, radicalism meant support for emancipation either as a means of suppressing the rebellion or as an end in itself. After the Emancipation Proclamation was issued in 1863, the resolution of the status and rights of the freedmen became a source of conflict between radicals and nonradicals, and when the war ended the treatment of former rebels and the readmission of the seceded states to the Union formed additional issues for factional strife. In the political struggles of the 1860s therefore intraparty division played a heightened role. Because of that alteration in the customary pattern of American politics, the problem of radicalism warrants consideration before examining the bearing of the slavery issue on the question of war aims.

Radicalism before the war consisted in the condemnation of slavery on moral grounds and the insistence on the ultimate extinction of slavery. An increasing number of Republicans affirmed these principles in the controversy over the extension of slavery into the territories, and when the Republican party refused to accept any compromise on the territorial question in the winter of 1860–61 it became for all practical purposes—at least in southern eyes—an abolition party. The question arises whether the party remained basically united on ideology and policy. Were the chief conflicts of Civil War politics, in other words, those between Republicans and Democrats, or did a fundamental division between radical and nonradical Republicans shape the most important political struggles of the war?

The latter view, more familiarly referred to as the controversy between Lincoln and the radicals, acknowledges that there was initial agreement on the border state strategy of assuming an attitude of restraint toward slavery to prevent the loyal slave states from joining the Confederacy. Early in the contest, however, proponents of this interpretation argue, radicals determined to revolutionize southern politics and society by confiscating rebel property, abolishing slavery, and imposing territorial governments on the defeated South. Historians who advance this thesis concede that the party united on the wisdom of abolishing slavery, but they stress that radicals wanted to employ remorseless, revolutionary violence to accomplish their more far-reaching ends. Doctrinaire in their pursuit of antislavery objectives and in their plan to establish congressional hegemony over the executive, the radicals, according to this view, profoundly divided the Republican party.[1]

More compelling reasons exist, however, for holding that the main line of conflict in Civil War politics was between a Republican party fundamentally united on both the objects of the war and the means of waging it, and their Democratic opponents. As the Republican party found unity prior to 1861 in efforts to stop the spread of slavery, so in the war years its unity rested on the commitment to preserve the Union. This policy might be seen as conservative insofar as it implicitly ignored slavery and accepted the possibility of its continuation. Historical developments proved otherwise, however, because the prewar Union, with slavery protected, in reality no longer existed.

With the advance and occupation of Union armies, changes began at the very outset that altered the political and legal environment of slavery. Calling escaped slaves contraband of war, General Benjamin F. Butler as early as May 1861 initiated a policy of providing the contrabands with employment and freedom within Union lines.[2] In August 1861 Congress passed a confiscation act, to be enforced in federal courts, which stated that southerners who employed slaves for hostile military purposes forfeited their claim to the slaves' labor. Together these measures suggested that the war would have an adverse effect on slavery. At the same time, moreover, Republicans disavowed any intention of overthrowing state institutions in the Crittenden-Johnson resolutions, and acknowledged that slavery might be destroyed as a result of the war.[3] Already the fugitive slave law, a conspicuous feature of the prewar Union, was falling into disuse after Congress passed a resolution releasing fed-

1. See T. Harry Williams, "Lincoln and the Radicals: An Essay in Civil War History and Historiography," in Grady McWhiney, ed., *Grant, Lee, Lincoln and the Radicals: Essays on Civil War Leadership* (Evanston, 1964), 92–117.

2. See below, p. 49ff., for a discussion of the freedman's policy following Butler's contraband tactic.

3. *Cong. Globe*, 37 Cong., 1 Sess., 259 (July 25, 1861), remarks of Ira Harris.

eral officers from responsibility to enforce the statute and federal commanders received escaped slaves within their lines.[4]

What was impressive about the Republican party was its rapid and on the whole unified advance to the conclusion that military emancipation was an indispensable means of preserving the Union. After prohibiting military officers from returning escaped slaves in March 1862, Republican lawmakers abolished slavery in the District of Columbia, prohibited it in the territories, and, in the Confiscation Act of 1862, recognized slaves of rebels entering Union lines as free persons. Concurrently they authorized the employment of emancipated slaves as soldiers and military laborers. Lincoln meanwhile adjusted to the quickened pace of congressional antislavery action. Within the framework of the border state strategy, he supported gradual, compensated emancipation, and then, in July 1862, began to formulate a policy of military emancipation. In September 1862 he revealed his new policy toward slavery in the preliminary Emancipation Proclamation.

The historical logjam over slavery once loosened, Republicans pressed the logic of the situation to a proper conclusion. Even if restoration of the old Union were possible, that outcome did not seem desirable because it was precisely the Union "as it was" that contained the seeds of the present conflict.[5] What this means is that the relationship between slavery and the American republic was in process of resolution. While this development would require several years, by the end of 1862 it clearly appeared that the war would severely damage slavery if not destroy it outright.

A variety of factors has obscured the ideological unity of the Republican party that sustained this historic resolution of the slavery question. In the first place, the departure of southern Democrats gave the Republicans an overwhelming majority in

4. Louis S. Gerteis, *From Contraband to Freedman: Federal Policy Toward Southern Blacks 1861–1865* (Westport, Conn., 1973), 14–15.

5. Carl Russell Fish, *The American Civil War* (New York, 1937), 312–13.

the Thirty-seventh Congress and naturally caused attention to focus on tensions within the dominant party. Perhaps a more important reason for emphasizing internal division within the Republican party has been the state-oriented nature of American politics. Like all political parties in the United States, the Republicans were a congeries of state parties whose members competed for the stakes of power that the federal system made available at the local level. To win election, moreover, politicians flexibly and expediently adopted now one policy, now another, according to their opponent's standpoint or some other adventitious circumstance.

In the case of Civil War Republicans, the decisive consideration in charting a course of action often became identification with or support of the Lincoln administration. Since the fairly even division between the parties required Lincoln to avoid extreme positions in order to build a broad base of support, the administration position invariably appeared conservative compared to the views of the militant antislavery wing of the party. Accordingly politicians who looked to the administration for assistance, as in the distribution of patronage, appeared as moderates or conservatives, while those who opposed them appeared as radicals.[6]

In addition to this purely political radicalism there existed what we may call ideological or conscience radicalism.[7] This term refers to the tendency of lawmakers and voters to act on the basis of principle, commitment, belief, and the perception of issues on their merits. Of course character and temperament— the elements of personality that dispose one to more or less precipitate action in pursuit of what he believes to be right— were also involved, and among Civil War Republicans this factor rather than basic ideological tenets distinguished radicals from nonradicals. Most Republicans endorsed radical objec-

6. Michael Les Benedict, *A Compromise of Principle: Congressional Republicans and Reconstruction*, 1863–1869 (New York, 1974), 59–69.

7. Ibid., 59.

tives, such as emancipation and guarantees for freedmen's rights, but they tended to be circumspect in pursuing them.[8] Instead of offering a separate program of their own, moderate and conservative Republicans represented points on a spectrum that registered differences in method, timing, and assessment of political reality, rather than differences in ideology and fundamental objectives.[9]

Failure properly to understand the nature of constitutional conflict, especially a tendency to view constitutional disputes as merely derivative of political and ideological differences, has also obscured the essential unity of the Republican outlook. Lincoln and Congress frequently clashed because of the inherent disposition to conflict in the separation of powers. The institutional structure, that is, rather than differences over principle or policy led to controversy. Despite agreement on policy, lawmakers often felt compelled to protect legislative prerogatives, as in the Habeas Corpus Act of 1863 or the Wade-Davis reconstruction bill of 1864. At the same time, identification in the public mind between conservative Republicans and the President to a considerable extent derived from this institutional antagonism between legislative and executive branches.[10]

Quantitative studies of Civil War legislative behavior have confirmed that Democratic-Republican rivalry exceeded intraparty division and that differences among Republicans turned more on temperament and constitutional outlook than on war aims and ideological principle. Perhaps the most significant finding is that radicals were not a small, isolated group of extremists who forced the majority to accept their views. Historians have identified a large number of radicals when defining radicalism as opposition to slavery, commitment to a vigorous war effort, hostility to the South and former rebels, and support for freedmen's rights. The earliest quantitative analyses, for example, concluded that well over half the Republican members

8. Ibid., 48–58.
9. Fish, *The American Civil War*, 312.
10. Ibid., 313–14.

of Congress were radical.[11] More refined measurement presents a spectrum of opinion on which individual Republicans appear at different points over a period of time, rather than a picture of static and monolithic radical and nonradical blocs. The number of radicals, however, remains high. One study places it at half of the Republican senators who adopted a consistent position from 1861 to 1866.[12] No deep chasm, writes historian Allan G. Bogue, but rather a system of interlocking fissures running in the same direction, describes the relationship between Republican factions in Congress.[13]

Republicans acted together far more than they divided along radical and moderate lines. In the Senate from 1861 to 1863, for example, Republicans followed party lines on 180 of 368 roll calls; on only 58 votes did a significant radical-moderate split occur. With respect to slavery and confiscation, which form perhaps the most important area for evaluating ideological cohesiveness, radical versus nonradical divisions occurred more frequently, on 21 of 87 roll calls or 24 percent of the time compared to 16 percent on all issues. Nevertheless, such internal division existed much less often than party unity against Democrats. When Republicans split along factional lines, moreover, constitutional attitudes received equal if not greater attention as sources of controversy than political sentiments such as punitive spirit toward the South and prejudice against blacks.[14]

11. Glenn M. Linden, " 'Radicals' and Economic Policies: The Senate, 1861–1873," *Journal of Southern History*, XXXII (May 1966), 188–99; Linden, " 'Radicals' and Economic Policies: The House of Representatives, 1861–1873," *Civil War History*, XIII (March 1967), 51–65; David Donald, *The Politics of Reconstruction 1863–1867* (Baton Rouge, 1965), 29–35.

12. Allan G. Bogue, "The Radical Voting Dimension in the U.S. Senate During the Civil War," *Journal of Interdisciplinary History*, III (Winter 1973), 449–74. This study identifies nine radicals, nine non-radicals, and eleven senators who fluctuated between radical and nonradical positions.

13. Allan G. Bogue, "The Substantive Meaning of Radicalism in the United States Senate During the Civil War," unpublished paper presented to the Organization of American Historians, April 1972, p. 5.

14. Ibid., pp. 28–37.

According to Bogue, radicals saw themselves as "in earnest," while moderates preferred to express their attitude in the phrase "men, money, and the Constitution."[15] Thus differences in political temperament, zeal, and constitutional outlook, rather than division over fundamental ideology and war aims, separated radical and nonradical blocs on those relatively few occasions when they failed to agree.

Republican ideological agreement notwithstanding, the question of war aims remained to be dealt with, and through it the fundamental issue of slavery in the American republic. Initially the matter seemed simple enough: the purpose of the war was to maintain the Constitution and the Union, and to restore the states with their rights and institutions intact. Yet the way the war would be conducted, the means chosen to suppress the rebellion, might have more to do with determining the purpose or end of the struggle than any profession of intentions, such as the Crittenden-Johnson resolutions of 1861.

The controversies that occurred over confiscation and emancipation in 1862 illustrate the means-end problem that lay at the heart of the war aims issue. Both confiscation and emancipation emerged primarily as expedient measures intended to weaken the enemy and strengthen the Union militarily. They may also be viewed, however, as measures that signified the adoption of war aims going beyond, and containing a moral and ideological dimension not present in, the original purpose of maintaining the Union. If slavery, according to this point of view, was the overriding moral issue before the war, then the decision for emancipation indicated an advance beyond Unionism to the higher ground of antislavery principle and ideology.

There is an unarticulated assumption in this view, however, that needs to be reexamined if we are to understand the relationship between emancipation and war aims. That assumption is the idea that Unionism lacked moral and ideological content. A closer look at Republican Unionism will show on the contrary that it contained a moral dimension identical to that which

15. Ibid., p. 43.

historians have more readily discerned in the emancipation policy. Instead of a two-stage progression of war aims from nationalistic reason-of-state to antislavery moral principle, there was in Republican war policy a continuous concern for both expediency and moral idealism in the defense of the Union and in the adoption of an emancipation policy. The result was that at the end of the war the prohibition of slavery in the Thirteenth Amendment represented an extension and fulfillment of the essentially moral idea of republican self-government that informed the Unionism of 1861.

While northern Unionism may be seen as expressing the same realistic nationalism that dominated European politics in the nineteenth century, it was heavily colored with, indeed was based upon, liberal moral and ideological principles. In this respect it was similar to previous conceptions of American nationality from the Revolution on. So far from being dependent on language, religion, culture, and historical tradition, as the national idea in Europe was, American nationality was defined by universal principles of natural rights individualism and self-government.[16] Although variations in the national idea were possible, a fact which the party conflicts of the 1790s and 1830s demonstrated, the dominant conception in the nineteenth century was the Jeffersonian view that the idea of American nationality was most truly expressed in institutions of local self-government or state rights, rather than of centralized sovereignty. Whether political leaders emphasized local self-government or central authority, however, the distinctive quality of American nationality in the political realm was its moral and ideological character.

In opposing proslavery state sovereignty doctrines in the 1850s, antislavery reformers viewed Unionism not as an end in itself but as a means of extending the universal values of liberty and self-government. Instead of preservation of the existing order, as in the previous generation, the Union idea was identi-

16. Yehoshua Arieli, *Individualism and Nationalism in American Ideology* (Baltimore, 1966), passim.

fied with aggressive stewardship for the improvement of American liberty. Accordingly the Republican party adopted a "free society" Unionism which exalted political and social individualism as the essence of the national idea.[17] Events of the 1850s showed slavery to be repugnant to the ideal of republican self-government, and when the South seceded in 1861 Republicans defended the Union as a guarantee of decentralized local liberty.[18]

As though in preparation for the crisis that was to begin in 1861, Lincoln throughout the 1850s stressed the relationship between Union and republican liberty. When the repeal of the Missouri Compromise made it possible for new lands to become slave territory, he protested that this action contradicted national principles of universal liberty. In the House Divided speech Lincoln identified the Union with freedom, and as the crisis deepened he repeatedly stated that the essence of the national idea was not simply independence but republican self-government based on the principle of universal liberty and equality.[19] In resisting secession, therefore, Lincoln and most Republicans understood that the Union cause contained a moral purpose and significance that transcended mere vindication of national existence. Lincoln summarized this view when he told Congress in July 1861 that the war was "a People's contest," waged to defend a government the object of which was to elevate the condition of men. More pointedly he stated that in suppressing the rebellion the Union was upholding its constitu-

17. Paul C. Nagel, *This Sacred Trust: American Nationality 1798–1898* (New York, 1971), 130–35; Major L. Wilson, "The Repressible Conflict: Seward's Concept of Progress and the Free-Soil Movement," *Journal of Southern History*, XXXVII (November 1971), 533–56; Eric Foner, *Free Soil, Free Labor, Free Men: The Ideology of the Republican Party Before the Civil War* (New York, 1970).

18. Phillip S. Paludan, "The American Civil War Considered as a Crisis in Law and Order," *American Historical Review*, LXXVII (October 1972), 1013–34.

19. Harry V. Jaffa, "Expediency and Morality in the Lincoln-Douglas Debates," *The Anchor Review*, no. 2 (1957), 179–204; Roy P. Basler et al., eds., *The Collected Works of Abraham Lincoln* (9 vols.; New Brunswick, 1953–55), IV, 3, 15–16, 193–94, 220, 231, 236, 240.

tional obligation to guarantee republican government to each state.[20]

From the outset the slavery issue entered into discussions of war aims. Fearful of the changes war could bring, Democrats sought approval of a resolution stating that Union armies would not subjugate states or abolish slavery. Republicans rejected all such propositions as superfluous, until the Union defeat at Bull Run in July 1861 made them more amenable to a conservative statement of aims. The result was the passage of the Crittenden-Johnson resolutions, which declared that the purpose of the war was to maintain the Union and the states, not to overthrow or interfere with their rights or institutions. The resolutions did not, however, expressly support slavery or restrict the use of the army in any legal sense. Thus men who anticipated antislavery results from the fighting could support them.

By December 1861 it was apparent that the slavery issue was assuming larger importance and that the question of war aims was by no means settled. House Republicans not only refused to affirm the Crittenden-Johnson statement of intentions, but also introduced confiscation and emancipation bills that reopened debate about the government's objectives in the war.

The purpose of confiscation at first seemed to be to weaken the enemy and strengthen the Union by raising money from the sale of confiscated property. It was a means of maintaining the Union. Thus Lyman Trumbull, impatient with uncertainty over the method by which confiscation should proceed, argued that the government must simply take the rebel property and sell it whether individual southerners came to trial or not.[21] Senator

20. Ibid., IV, 438–40.
21. *Cong. Globe*, 37 Cong., 2 Sess., 1959 (May 6, 1862). A major issue in the confiscation debate was whether the government could treat rebels as enemies and take their property summarily, either by military seizure or the legal action of *in rem* proceedings against the property itself, or whether participants in the rebellion must be treated as citizens of the United States entitled to guarantees of the Constitution, including the right not to be deprived of life, liberty, or property without due process of law. For an excellent analysis of this problem see Patricia

Lot M. Morrill of Maine urged immediate seizure and sale of rebel property to aid the Union effort, while Thomas D. Eliot of Massachusetts described the taking of enemies' property as a legitimate instrument of war.[22]

A thoroughgoing confiscation policy, however, especially if accompanied by emancipation,[23] would go far beyond restoring the Union. It would profoundly alter the political and social condition of the seceded states, and perhaps even cause changes in the federal system. In other words, as a means of suppressing the rebellion, confiscation might in fact repudiate the avowed aim of restoring the states to their prewar standing. Looked at in this way, confiscation might be more useful as a feature of *postwar* policy toward the rebel states and toward individual southerners, rather than as an element of wartime policy.

Although radicals evinced an interest in the emerging reconstruction problem at this time,[24] nonradicals more often approached confiscation in postwar policy terms. Encouraged by Union victories in the west and reacting against radical urging of direct military seizure of property as an instrument of war, several moderate and conservative Republicans in early 1862 proposed to confiscate property in postwar judicial proceedings against individuals convicted of treason or rebellion. Such a policy, intended to deal with punishment of rebels as a reconstruction problem, would respect the constitutional requirement of a jury trial in criminal prosecutions. Also, in con-

---

L. M. Lucie, "Confiscation: Constitutional Crossroads," *Civil War History*, XXIII (December 1977), 307–21.

22. *Cong. Globe*, 37 Cong., 2 Sess., 1897 (May 1, 1862), remarks of Lot M. Morrill, 2235–36 (May 20, 1862), remarks of Thomas D. Eliot.

23. Although most confiscation bills contained emancipation provisions, slaves were not considered to be property and were not to be confiscated like real or personal property. They were, however, considered along with property in the argument which held that under the war power the government could seize property and destroy the master-slave relationship enjoyed by rebels. Cf. *Cong. Globe*, 37 Cong., 2 Sess., Appendix 211 (May 26, 1862), remarks of Luther Hanchett.

24. See Herman Belz, *Reconstructing the Union: Theory and Policy during the Civil War* (Ithaca, 1969), 40–65.

trast to radical reconstruction bills proposing to treat the seceded states as territories, it would recognize the existence of the states and the pre-existing federal system. What was needed, said Senator Jacob Collamer of Vermont, a leading advocate of confiscation for reconstruction purposes, was a measure stern enough to make the defeated rebels apprehensive but one that was also realistically enforceable and not so draconian as to deny southerners a motive to return to allegiance. A confiscation act that punished the guilty and protected the innocent would promote the restoration of the Union.[25]

The Confiscation Act of 1862 contained elements of both a radical wartime and a more moderate postwar outlook. Lyman Trumbull's initial Senate bill called for military seizure and appropriation of the property of persons engaging in rebellion. Upon commission of the act of forfeiture, all right, title, and claim of an individual to property would become vested in the United States, and his slaves would be emancipated.[26] This extreme measure, which would have confiscated a vast amount of southern property, was intended to promote the war effort. It is apparent, however, that it would produce drastic changes in the South and thus go far toward a radical reconstruction of southern society.[27] Nonradicals, however, who justified confiscation as a punishment for the crime of rebellion, proposed to take property and emancipate slaves only after a court of law determined individual guilt[28] Nonradicals were willing to allow

25. *Cong. Globe*, 37 Cong., 2 Sess., 1809–11 (April 24, 1862). See also ibid., 1895 (May 1, 1862), remarks of Henry Wilson, Appendix, 197 (May 23, 1862), remarks of John Shanks, Appendix, 218–19 (May 24, 1862), remarks of B. F. Thomas, 1653 (April 14, 1862), remarks of Ira Harris, 2040–42 (May 20, 1862), remarks of Albert G. Riddle, 1769 (April 22, 1862), remarks of Eliakim Walton.

26. Ibid., 942 (February 25, 1862), S. No. 151; John Syrett, "The Confiscation Acts: Efforts at Reconstruction during the Civil War," Ph.D. dissertation, University of Wisconsin, 1971, p. 26.

27. See Syrett, "The Confiscation Acts," 1–4, 26, for a discussion of the reconstruction implications of immediate wartime confiscation measures.

28. *Cong. Globe*, 37 Cong., 2 Sess., 1814 (April 14, 1862), remarks of Jacob Collamer.

the President to seize and use rebel property temporarily to assist in suppressing the rebellion, but their major concern was to establish a sound postwar policy that, under judicial supervision, would punish the leaders of the rebellion.[29]

The Confiscation Act of 1862 was a compromise between these two approaches. It provided for judicial implementation of confiscation by civil proceedings against rebel property (that is, *in rem* proceedings) instead of either by direct military means or through individual criminal conviction. The act directed the President to seize the property of six classes of rebels, and of all others who after sixty days notice refused to return to allegiance. The government might use occupied or seized property for revenue purposes, but to get title it must institute proceedings (as in admiralty or revenue cases) against the property of persons engaging in rebellion, in federal district courts where the property was located. If the property was found to belong to a person engaged in rebellion, it was to be condemned as enemies' property and become the property of the United States. These provisions gave the radicals what they most wanted, viz., a method of proceeding against property that bypassed criminal trial and conviction of individual owners. On the other hand, the act satisfied important nonradical demands by requiring the use of judicial process which it appeared would not become operative until federal courts were reestablished in the South after the war, by restricting confiscation to only six classes of rebels, and by entrusting enforcement to the executive.[30]

Insofar as temporary use of lands seized under the confiscation act might through crops and rents provide revenues to

29. Ibid.

30. Syrett, "The Confiscation Acts," 83–84. The act of July 17, 1862 contained a treason section which authorized confiscation of property for payment of a $10,000 fine and emancipation of slaves as punishment after trial and conviction. The central feature of the act, however, was the provision for confiscation without criminal trial.

It should be noted that, contrary to expectation in 1862, the Union government created provost courts under military authority to deal with civil and criminal law in the occupied South, and also a Provisional Court in Louisiana.

sustain the war effort, the measure could be seen as compatible with the original aim of preserving the Union. To the extent that it anticipated postwar proceedings against rebel property it acquired a reconstruction character and suggested possible redefinition of war aims. Despite the emphasis in congressional debate on the military pertinence of the act, it was the postwar aspect that stood out more clearly. In arguing for confiscation as a war measure, supporters spoke only in the most general terms, and several Republicans dismissed outright the notion that the act would bring money into the treasury.[31] This prediction proved largely correct, because the confiscation provisions could be enforced only in the North, where federal courts were operating.[32]

On the other hand, as a reconstruction measure the confiscation act raised the possibility of achieving results—such as widespread redistribution of rebel property and slave emancipation—that would preclude restoration of the states to their prewar standing. It would thus prevent restoration of the Union as it was. Yet this radical outcome was by no means assured. The most important reason was that Lincoln persuaded Congress to accept his view that the confiscation act should not be interpreted to permit forfeiture of real estate beyond the lifetime of the offender.[33] This qualification restricted the radical potential of the act, so that its chief significance for reconstruction consisted in the procedure it offered for punishing rebel leaders and inducing rank and file southerners to return to allegiance. A section authorizing the President to extend pardon and amnesty to persons engaged in rebellion reflected the moderate reconstruction purpose that characterized the confiscation act.[34] Of the two alternatives that radicals believed existed—namely,

31. Syrett, "The Confiscation Acts," 54–55.

32. James G. Randall, *Constitutional Problems Under Lincoln*, rev. ed. (Urbana, 1951), 291, reports that $300,000 was realized as proceeds from confiscation sales.

33. Ibid., 280.

34. *Cong. Globe*, 37 Cong., 2 Sess., Appendix, 413, Confiscation act, sec. 13, July 17, 1862.

passage of a law producing immediate benefit for the war effort
or one that looked to the trial and conviction of leading rebels
after the restoration of peace[35]—Congress inclined towards the
latter.

If the debate over confiscation involved consideration of
war aims, emancipation proposals in 1862 raised the issue even
more clearly and directly. Much as Republicans wanted to defeat the enemy and reconstruct the South, their commitment to
private property complicated and inhibited their approach to
confiscation.[36] No such restraints operated, however, in relation to the slavery question. Although Republicans disagreed on
the timing and constitutional method of antislavery action, in
substantive policy terms they were fundamentally united on this
issue, just as before the war they had agreed on the objective of
stopping the spread of slavery. In the wartime context, however,
Republicans regarded antislavery action as a means of preserving the Union rather than an end in itself. Indeed this view of
the matter justified the abandonment of the fundamental constitutional principle that the federal government lacked power to
interfere with slavery in the states where it existed. At the same
time, however, Republican emancipation policy, though theoretically consistent with the narrow aim of suppressing the rebellion, expressed the party's historic purpose of ending slavery in
America. It thus portended a changed Union.

Congress took up emancipation in an instrumental way
almost simultaneously with its affirmation of the exclusive purpose of maintaining the Union and preserving the rights and
institutions of the states. Although the Crittenden-Johnson resolutions of July 1861 did not expressly refer to slavery, they
were generally assumed to imply that slavery as a state institution would be protected in the restored Union. In the first confiscation act, however, passed a fortnight later, Congress treated
emancipation as a means of conducting the war. The act de-

35. *Independent*, Washington correspondence, May 1, 1862.
36. Leonard P. Curry, *Blue Print for Modern America: Nonmilitary
Legislation of the First Civil War Congress* (Nashville, 1968), 99.

clared forfeit all claims to the labor of slaves who were employed in military efforts in support of the rebellion.[37] Although it was a cautious enough step, which avoided a declaration of slave freedom lest Congress appear to be attacking slavery as a state institution, the act raised the possibility that reliance on antislavery means might in fact be more important for determining war aims than resolutions about preserving the Union as it was.

Congress adopted a series of antislavery acts in 1862. It barred the military from returning fugitive slaves, prohibited slavery in territories of the United States, and abolished slavery in the District of Columbia. Minor though these measures were, they suggested that the Union "as it was" no longer in fact existed, and that if slavery should survive it would be gravely weakened. Nevertheless, the failure of Congress in its emancipation legislation of 1862 to guarantee freed slaves personal liberty and ordinary civil rights such as owning property, making contracts, bringing suit, and testifying in court, showed that it regarded slave liberation as a military and political expedient rather than a moral and humanitarian reform for the benefit of the Negro slave population.[38]

Although a few Republicans showed awareness of the civil rights problem that the freedmen would face, the Confiscation Act of 1862—the outstanding antislavery accomplishment of the session—contained no procedure for guaranteeing emancipated slaves' personal liberty and rights.[39] The act declared

37. The act was directed against property and slave labor, rather than rebellious individuals, and was to be enforced by *in rem* proceedings in federal district courts. Randall, *Constitutional Problems Under Lincoln*, 276.

38. Herman Belz, "Protection of Personal Liberty in Republican Emancipation Legislation of 1862," *Journal of Southern History*, XLII (August 1976), 385–400.

39. The act abolishing slavery in the District of Columbia contained an emancipation procedure that resulted in the award of a certificate of freedom for former slaves. Also the House of Representatives passed an emancipation bill which gave freed slaves the protection of the writ of habeas corpus against subsequent detention. This provision was rejected in the final formulation of the confiscation act.

slaves of rebels who came within Union lines, or were found in places occupied by Union armies, to be "captives of war" and forever free. It provided no means, however, of implementing the liberty it proclaimed. In effect the act confirmed the actual emancipation that occurred as Union armies advanced, and reflected military expediency rather than humanitarian purpose. Its significance, in the words of an antislavery correspondent, lay in the fact that it "authorizes the President to make any use he pleases of black men, bound or free, in this struggle. . . . Congress has solemnly asked the President . . . *to use the black man in this war!* This is something."[40]

The Lincoln administration also defended emancipation as an expedient military measure rather than as a new, ideologically inspired war aim. At the outset, as we have seen, the necessity of keeping the border states loyal led to a policy of restraint toward slavery. Although Lincoln acquiesced in Benjamin F. Butler's contraband policy of employing escaped slaves in military labor and approved the first confiscation act, he repudiated General John C. Frémont's emancipation order in Missouri. Within the framework of a cautious border state policy, however, he showed signs of adjustment to the growing antislavery sentiment in Congress when he advised voluntary state emancipation in December 1861 and proposed a formal plan for gradual, compensated emancipation in March 1862. To give the plan a chance of success Lincoln again negated a military commander's emancipation order, and he specially appealed to border state representatives for support. These efforts failed, however, leaving little practical alternative but to move toward all-out emancipation.

Historians have debated at length the nature of Lincoln's decision to support emancipation. The prevalent view in recent years has been that Lincoln determined upon emancipation for politico-military reasons in mid-1862, when it became clear that the border state policy would not succeed, but postponed imple-

40. *Independent*, July 17, 1862. The act authorized the President to employ blacks in military labor.

menting it until a Union victory would enable him to appear to be acting out of strength rather than weakness. Accounts also stress that Lincoln delayed emancipation until northern public opinion was prepared for it.[41]

One may doubt, however, that Lincoln's mind was entirely made up by July 1862 and that timing was his only consideration thereafter. The first emancipation paper he drafted in July, for example, differed noticeably from the proclamations he issued later. Warning all persons to return to allegiance or suffer forfeiture of property under the confiscation act, the draft proclamation of July reiterated Lincoln's proposal for compensated state emancipation and declared slaves in rebel states free.[42] Lincoln not only refrained from publishing this order, however; he also stated, in answer to Horace Greeley's "Prayer of Twenty Millions," that slavery was a secondary consideration to Unionism. When he actually issued the preliminary Emancipation Proclamation, after the repulse at Antietam and before a meeting of Republican governors, he did so primarily for the political reason of maintaining the backing of radicals while deflating their popular appeal.[43]

It has become a commonplace of American historiography to point out, lest the popular conception of Lincoln as the great emancipator be taken too seriously, that the Emancipation Proclamation rested on strictly pragmatic grounds and applied only to Confederate territory not under Union control, so that it actually freed no slaves.[44] From a different perspective it has become almost equally commonplace to conclude that the proclamation of freedom constituted an additional war aim that signified a higher moral purpose than mere defense of the

41. V. Jacque Voegeli, *Free but Not Equal: The Midwest and the Negro during the Civil War* (Chicago, 1967), 40–41.

42. Basler, ed., *Collected Works of Lincoln*, V, 336–37.

43. James C. Welling, "The Emancipation Proclamation," *North American Review*, CXXX (February 1880), 163–85; William B. Hesseltine, *Lincoln and the War Governors* (New York, 1948), 249–72.

44. Richard Hofstadter, *The American Political Tradition and the Men Who Made It* (New York, 1948), 93–136, especially at 132–33, is the classic statement of this demythologizing conclusion.

Union.[45] Certainly in its narrow wartime context the expedient nature of the proclamation stood out: plainly it was necessary to strengthen the political base required to support the military struggle. Yet it is also true that the Emancipation Proclamation was a response to historical necessity, and that in this broader perspective it embodied the basic antislavery purpose of the Republican party and also the moral and ideological elements in Unionism. When we examine the matter in this light, we see that emancipation was both means and end, and that political expediency and ideological principle were inextricably linked in both the defense of the Union and the decision for emancipation.

The unifying factor in Republican policy, the common denominator between the initial aim of defending the Union and the instrumental use of emancipation, was the principle of republicanism. As noted previously, the North went to war not simply out of a kind of natural instinct to preserve the life of the nation, but consciously to maintain a national union defined by republican liberty. Government operating through majority rule and founded on the idea that all men were created equal, so that none should be governed without his consent, was the basis of the republican system that northerners identified with the Constitution and the Union. This identification not only made defense of the Union a moral and ideological cause, it gave Unionism the same moral rationale that sustained the movement against slavery.

Slavery could of course be condemned on a variety of grounds, but the most pertinent from the Republican standpoint was its utter contradiction of the principle of consent. However it may have been modulated within the private household, slavery was a public system of command—a form of legal and political rule—that denied virtually an entire race of people the right of participation and consent in their own governance.

45. See Mark L. Krug, "The Republican Party and the Emancipation Proclamation," *Journal of Negro History*, XLVIII (April 1963), 98–114.

Though loath to regard blacks as political or social equals, Republicans nevertheless insisted on their equality with other men in respect of personal liberty. Enjoyment of this right would at least enable blacks to partake of republican self-government in its most elementary form, viz., control of oneself without interference from another. Before participation in the political community could be attained, this primordial and ir-reducible level of self-government must be realized. The prag-matic and prudential considerations that went into it notwith-standing, the decision for emancipation expressed this moral and ideological purpose.[46]

Shortly before deciding on emancipation in September 1862, Lincoln discussed the bearing that such a policy would have on the question of war aims. A group of antislavery clergymen, in conference with the President, took the view that emancipation should be adopted as a public affirmation that the war was being fought for more than national pride and ambi-tion, and that "a glorious principle" justified the North's strug-gle. Lincoln agreed on the usefulness of emancipation, but denied that it would give the Union cause a moral dimension previously lacking. "I think you should admit," he said, "that we already have an important principle to rally and unite the people in the fact that constitutional government is at stake. This is a fundamental idea, going about as deep as anything."[47] Lincoln's visitors accepted this point but insisted that slave emancipation and defense of the Union were inseparably con-nected. Constitutional government was "a grand idea," they replied, "but the people know that *nothing else put constitu-tional government in danger but slavery*." They held further that the aristocratic and despotic element of slavery was "the incon-

46. On the relationship between the antislavery movement and re-publicanism, see generally Harry V. Jaffa, *Crisis of the House Divided: An Interpretation of the Issues in the Lincoln-Douglas Debates* (Seattle, 1973; originally published in 1959), and Jaffa, "The Emancipation Proclamation," in R. A. Goldwin, ed., *100 Years of Emancipation* (Chi-cago, 1964), 1–24.

47. Basler, ed., *Collected Works of Lincoln*, V, 423–24.

sistency that had nearly wrought our ruin and caused free government to appear a failure before the world. . . ."[48]

The argument was persuasive, and Lincoln acknowledged its force. Indeed it was the very argument he himself had made in decrying the danger of slavery in the 1850s. Accordingly, when his visitors explained the matter thus, Lincoln interjected to say, "Yes, that is the true ground of our difficulties."[49] Emancipation was thus an expedient answer to the immediate politico-military problems facing the government, and in a moral and ideological sense a correct solution to the fundamental issue of slavery and the American republic.

The principles of republicanism underlying both Unionism and emancipation have perhaps not been properly appreciated because of a too literal acceptance of Lincoln's assertion that the Emancipation Proclamation was based on military necessity. To be sure, the proclamation had important military results, even if its political consequences mattered most initially. In 1863 the army recruited large numbers of blacks, most of them former slaves, and by the middle of 1864 Lincoln stated that without this force of approximately 140,000 black soldiers, sailors, and laborers the government could no longer continue the contest.[50] Without denying the contribution blacks made to the Union cause, however, one may be permitted to doubt that Lincoln's estimate was entirely sound, or that the white population would have been unable to supply an equivalent force.[51] The fact is Lincoln emphasized military necessity because in constitutional and political terms the logic of emancipation required it.

Denial of federal power over slavery in the states where it existed was so firmly established in constitutional law that it was necessary to use a legal fiction—the military necessity of emancipation—to justify and legitimize the revolutionary fed-

48. Ibid.
49. Ibid.
50. Lincoln to Charles D. Robinson, August 17, 1864, ibid., VII, 499–500.
51. Fish, *The American Civil War*, 326.

eral intervention that occurred. This does not mean that military considerations were irrelevant. The principal reason, however, for arguing military necessity was to sanction federal emancipation of slaves and reconcile this result with existing constitutional and legal premises. In other words, the argument from military necessity was intended, like legal fictions in general, to escape the consequences of an existing specific rule of law while at the same time explaining a new development in terms consistent with an existing conceptual framework.[52] Paradoxically, reliance on extraordinary military power, the antithesis of constituted civil authority, made possible continued adherence to traditional federalism.

Legal fictions are also used to avoid giving the real reasons for certain actions.[53] In the case of emancipation we may conclude that the real reason for it, considered in broad historical perspective, was hostility to slavery based on commitment to republicanism and the principle of equality on which republicanism rested. Anti-Negro prejudice in the North, however, made it politically inexpedient to justify emancipation in these positive moral and ideological terms. For the sake of border state and southern Unionist sensibilities, moreover, which continued to weigh heavily in Lincoln's thinking, it was desirable to avoid the appearance of relying on the elevated principles of antislavery reform. A more useful legal rationalization was the argument from military necessity, which could be seen as involving nothing more than suppression of the rebellion. Politically as well as constitutionally, therefore, it was necessary publicly to justify emancipation not on radical moral and ideological considerations but on the more conservative legalistic ground of military expediency. Lincoln's strict adherence to this legal fiction should not obscure the very real element of principle that the Emancipation Proclamation contained.[54]

52. Lon L. Fuller, "Legal Fictions," *Northwestern University Law Review*, XXV (January 1931), 513–46.
53. Harold J. Berman, "Legal Reasoning," *International Encyclopedia of the Social Sciences* (17 vols.; New York, 1968), IX, 203.
54. Don E. Fehrenbacher, "Only His Stepchildren: Lincoln and the Negro," *Civil War History*, XX (December 1974), 306.

"As a fit and necessary war measure for suppressing the rebellion" therefore, and by virtue of his authority as commander-in-chief, Lincoln issued the Emancipation Proclamation on January 1, 1863.[55] Preservation of the Union thus remained the official aim of the war that a policy of military emancipation would implement.

In political reality, however, if not in legal fact, the purpose of the war had been enlarged to include antislavery reform. The confiscation debate had provided a forum for considering the question of war aims in 1862. With radicals emphasizing property seizure as a tool of war and moderates viewing it as a beginning step in reconstruction, the confiscation act was a compromise that held out the possibility of a reconstructed rather than simply a restored Union. Emancipation affected the question of war aims in a more decisive way. Initiated as a military measure for suppressing the rebellion, it became an additional war aim. As defense of the Union involved both republican principle and pragmatic considerations of national survival, so emancipation rested on republican principles of antislavery reform as well as the politico-military exigencies of the wartime situation.

55. Basler, ed., *Collected Works of Lincoln*, VI, 29.

3

The Status of the Freedmen

Beginning of a National Policy

FROM THE VERY BEGINNING of the war, and in ever larger numbers as Union armies advanced, slaves acquired actual freedom. As they did, the future of the Negro people in America came sharply into focus. The Union government at first considered the ex-slaves contraband of war, somewhere between slavery and freedom. The Confiscation Act of 1862, however, declared slaves escaping from rebel masters captives of war and forever free, and the Emancipation Proclamation went further, asserting that all slaves in unoccupied rebellious states were free. While these measures cleared away much of the uncertainty surrounding the contraband theory, they only pointed in the general direction of greater liberty for emancipated slaves. The precise status and rights of the freedmen remained undetermined. On the front lines Union military officers were taking action concerning hundreds of thousands of liberated slaves that resolved in at least a minimal way the question of their status. Meanwhile, in an arena that at times seemed equally chaotic, Congress struggled to develop a national policy toward the freedmen.

Blacks responded with alacrity to war-created opportunities for freedom, asserting themselves in ways that influenced the policies of the Union government. Far from being an inert social mass merely to be acted upon, they fought for their freedom by taking up arms and by engaging in a variety of political actions.[1] Still, the principal responsibility for action lay with the emancipators. The central question was: what disposition should the Union government make of the freed slave population?

Two basic approaches, both having roots in the antecedent slavery struggle, came into conflict in dealing with the issue. On the one hand there was a strong tendency to let emancipated slaves alone on the theory, partly inspired by abolitionist teaching, that they could take care of themselves like any other group of people. Nineteenth century doctrines of laissez-faire reinforced this hands-off, minimum government approach. On the other hand, the actual circumstances in which the freedmen found themselves—the result of both slavery and the ravages of war—seemed to require that the government assume a guardian-like role in relation to emancipated slaves. Lending reinforcement to such a role were the sense of moral responsibility that many Unionists believed was inherent in the act of emancipation, and the common sense perception that the destruction of slavery as a labor system necessitated the formation of new civil arrangements.

Theoretical considerations aside, the immediate problems were immense. To begin with, there was the need to care for the physical wants of hundreds of thousands of escaped slaves. Under the circumstances, with sometimes as many as thirty thousand refugee blacks pouring into Union lines, as after the battle of Vicksburg, suffering and misery were unavoidable. Beyond the sheer contingency of events, military requirements prevented Union officials from dealing with the results of emancipation. The relief and safeguarding of freed slaves were necessarily secondary to the army's effectiveness. Another consideration in freedmen's policy was the need for continued cultivation and sale of cotton for the purpose of aiding the Union treasury and supplying northern textile mills with raw

1. Cf. James M. McPherson, *The Negro's Civil War: How American Negroes Felt and Acted During the War for the Union* (New York, 1965).

materials. These immediate concerns merged with longer range issues. The South's economy needed to be revived; the government must reunite the nation while allaying popular apprehensions about changes in race relations; emancipated slaves needed to be integrated into civil society and helped to become self-supporting and independent. In dealing with the exigencies of war Union officials, with considerable self-consciousness, determined basic directions in the development of the freed people.

Although all federal policies toward freedmen in the occupied South regarded the former slaves as an agricultural labor force, there were important variations according to local circumstances in southeastern Virginia, which was occupied in 1861 far from the front lines; on the all-black Sea Islands of South Carolina, when abolitionists came in 1861 to help the slaves to freedom; in the west; and in the central South.

In southeastern Virginia and northeastern North Carolina the freedmen's question was more easily separable from military considerations, and for that reason policy in these areas reflected more clearly than in other parts of the South northern preferences for dealing with the results of emancipation. Fewer practical difficulties concerning the status of escaped slaves arose in Virginia and North Carolina because slave owners generally fled, leaving federal authorities little choice but to accept responsibility for the slaves who remained.[2] Union freedmen's policy began in May 1861 with General Benjamin F. Butler's order declaring that the escaped slaves who had been used to build enemy fortifications were contraband of war and were not to be returned to disloyal owners. Soon Butler was receiving escaped slaves generally, employing them in camp labor at Fort Monroe. In 1862 under another commander, a plan to employ freedmen communally, with wages going into a fund for the support of destitute blacks, failed. The introduction of cash wages also brought no improvement because of fraud

2. Mary F. Berry, *Black Resistance/White Law: A History of Constitutional Racism in America* (New York, 1971), 82; Bell I. Wiley, *Southern Negroes 1861–1865* (New Haven, 1965; orig. publ. 1938), 181.

and mismanagement. In 1863, however, with General Butler again in command, freedmen's affairs assumed a more favorable outlook. Butler employed the majority of emancipated slaves on abandoned farms under contracts that secured them wages, food, clothing, and medical care, and he allowed a number of blacks to occupy rebel lands under sharecropping arrangements. Union authorities hoped that a vanguard of the freed people supported in this way would be able to change southern society and agriculture sufficiently to permit the mass of former slaves to become self-supporting free laborers.[3] By the end of the war Union policy in Virginia and North Carolina provided useful assistance to about sixty thousand freedmen, for which it won the praise of antislavery radicals.[4]

On the Sea Islands of South Carolina there was similar trial and error. For a while the contraband population worked for wages on government-run plantations, under the supervision of northern reformers. Later some ex-slaves were allowed to occupy abandoned lands as sharecroppers. In 1863, under pressure from northern entrepreneurs, the government-owned lands were offered for sale, thus allowing a more explicitly laissez faire, free labor approach. Although the land sales were intended to create a property-owning Negro peasantry, little was accomplished on this score because the principal purchasers were northern businessmen. Regarding the army's labor policy as too paternalistic, these businessmen employed Negro labor under contracts for wages or a share of the crop. They believed a self-help approach, based on the assumption that blacks could take care of themselves, was the surest route to social progress. In 1865 the government again tried the alternative of installing freedmen on the land, and General William T. Sherman settled forty thousand blacks under possessory titles along the South Carolina and Georgia coast. Although this land was restored to its owners under President Johnson, events in South Carolina demonstrated the ability of the freedmen, Union officials, and

3. Louis S. Gerteis, *From Contraband to Freedman: Federal Policy Toward Southern Blacks 1861–1865* (Westport, 1973), 33.
4. Ibid., 33–40.

benevolent reformers and businessmen to develop new forms of social organization based on free labor.[5]

The western war theater offered a more difficult situation in which to formulate post-emancipation policy. To begin with, since slave owners generally did not flee but professed loyalty and sought government protection of their property, the status of escaped slaves entering Union lines was a practical issue. The fugitive slave law was not automatically a dead letter, as it was in most of the east. Army-contraband relations in the west were also more problematic because the number of blacks involved was much larger than in the east.

Union occupation of New Orleans began in April 1862 with a policy of returning escaped slaves to their masters. By summer Congress reversed this policy, declaring that escaped slaves should be declared free. Radical antislavery pressure within the Department of the Gulf was an additional impetus for Union authorities to start planning free labor and Negro military recruitment policies. At a time when many slaves were leaving plantations for towns and cities, Union officials authorized their employment under government-supervised contracts either for loyal former masters or directly for the government itself. The standard contract was $10 per month pay (of which $3 could be in clothing), plus food and medical care in return for faithful and obedient labor for a year's time. In 1863 General Nathaniel P. Banks tightened the system by making freedmen's labor compulsory. Freedmen not employed on farms or by the army were required to live on what were called home colonies, supervised by the army, and to labor on public works projects for food, clothing, and shelter. Conspicuously they received no pay.[6]

Even when northern reformers played the supervisory role, as at Port Royal, South Carolina, labor relationships often bore an uncomfortable similarity to antebellum labor arrangements. In Louisiana Banks's anomalous policy of compulsory free

5. Willie Lee Rose, *Rehearsal for Reconstruction: The Port Royal Experiment* (Indianapolis, 1964), passim.

6. Gerteis, *From Contraband to Freedman*, 65–98.

labor was too transparently like the old regime to be acceptable, and blacks resisted it. They refused to work, left plantations, and often violently challenged white authority, both public and private. In response Banks sought to improve labor conditions, controlling planter-employers more closely to make sure they paid the freedmen, and starting a school system for emancipated slaves. Schools pleased the freedmen, who placed education high on their list of demands, and they also helped to maintain social order and promote the government's agricultural program by improving morale. Education was a means moreover of introducing northern values to former slaves, especially a free labor work ethic.[7]

The Mississippi valley, comprising Tennessee, Arkansas, and Mississippi, constituted yet another focal point for the development of freedmen's policy. In late 1862 the War Department established contraband camps under the direction of Colonel John Eaton. Army movements made accommodation of the great number of escaped slaves difficult, and few freedmen could be employed in military labor. So great was the burden of refugees that even the benevolent societies, which were dedicated to aiding the ex-slaves, feared the contraband population might have a negative effect on the performance of Union arms. Under these circumstances a contract labor system that would employ freed blacks on plantations, keeping them out of the wretched contraband camps, was an alternative favored by the most enlightened antislavery opinion.[8] Thus labor arrangements by which blacks worked under contract for wages characterized federal policy in the Mississippi valley and Louisiana.

Meanwhile the government undertook more systematically to utilize the black manpower becoming available to the Union. In 1862 Congress tried to move the administration in this direction by authorizing the employment of Negroes as military la-

7. William F. Messner, "Black Education in Louisiana, 1863–1865," *Civil War History*, XXII (March 1976), 41–59.

8. Gerteis, *From Contraband to Freedman*, 119–21; Allan Nevins, *The War for the Union* (4 vols.; New York, 1959–71), III, 427–29.

borers and soldiers. Lincoln agreed to the first of these propositions but not the second. By the end of the year, however, he allowed a few black regiments to be formed in the occupied South, and in the Emancipation Proclamation he announced that the government would accept freed slaves for garrison duty. In May 1863 the War Department created a Bureau of Colored Troops to supervise the all-out recruitment of southern Negroes as part of the administration's evolving freedmen's policy.

Under General Lorenzo Thomas, Union policy in the Mississippi valley in 1863 offered several options for emancipated slaves to follow. Blacks might enlist as soldiers; accept employment as military laborers; contract with private employers to work on plantations; or live under government supervision on home farms. Thomas's purposes were to relieve the army of the expense of caring for the freedmen, remove the freedmen from the contraband camps and place them in useful occupations, and revive the local economy to the benefit of the Union. Offering very low wages ($7 per month for men and $5 for women) Thomas declared that the war altered the tenure and conditions of black labor but not its necessity.[9]

The awakening of interest in reconstruction that accompanied the advance of federal armies in 1863 gave political significance to the Banks and Thomas labor systems. In the opinion of many antislavery reformers the government's policies toward emancipated slaves in Louisiana and the Mississippi valley were little better than slavery. Although some military officers, such as General Rufus Saxton in South Carolina, had the reputation of being pro-Negro, reformers generally viewed army officers as callous and indifferent toward the freedmen. For improvement in freedmen's affairs they looked to the Treasury Department, headed by radical Salmon P. Chase, which under the Direct Tax Act of 1862 and the Captured and Abandoned Property Act of 1863 had taken over the management of rebel

9. General Thomas, Order No. 9, March 11, 1864; R. N. Scott et al., eds., *The War of the Rebellion: A Compilation of the Official Records of the Union and Confederate Armies* (130 vols.; Washington, 1880–1901), Ser. III, vol. IV, 166–69.

plantations.[10] Since the ex-slaves needed land it seemed logical to bring them under Treasury Department regulations along with abandoned and confiscated property. Accordingly, in the winter of 1863–64 Treasury officials, supported by radical congressmen and reformers who favored a more paternalistic approach toward the matter, tried to gain control of freedmen's policy. Their chief aims were to ameliorate the contract labor system by raising wages (to $25 and $18 per month for men and women) and ultimately to eliminate it entirely by installing a substantial number of blacks on the land in rental or share-cropping arrangements.[11]

Both the War and Treasury Departments presented good arguments for control of the former slaves. While some army officers were cruel and insensitive toward blacks and military exigencies at times made it necessary to act with scant regard to their interests, many officers and men treated them humanely. The fact was, moreover, that only the army could provide physical protection for the freedmen. Furthermore, although necessarily exercising much control over the emancipated slaves, the army became identified with a minimal-government, laissez faire approach to freedmen's policy. Treasury agents, on the other hand, at least in the antislavery press, appeared as more sympathetic and fair toward blacks. Yet the commercial interests for which the Treasury was responsible often came into conflict with the interests of the freedmen, and it was evident that fraud, corruption, and mean-spiritedness were present among civilian as well as military officials. Perhaps most important, the Treasury Department was unable to protect the freed slaves against guerrilla attacks. Finally, because of its political

10. The first of these measures provided for the collection of direct taxes in rebel states, on default of landowners to pay the tax, through forfeiture of the land to the United States and sale at tax auctions. The captured and abandoned property act authorized the Treasury Department to take possession of miscellaneous property and abandoned plantations.

11. Louis S. Gerteis, "Salmon P. Chase, Radicalism, and the Politics of Emancipation, 1861–1864," *Journal of American History*, LX (June, 1973), 42–62.

tie with the freedmen's aid societies, the Treasury Department endorsed a more paternalistic approach to post-emancipation policy.

Competition between the War and Treasury Departments for control of freedmen's policy came to a head in early 1864. The previous autumn, in accordance with the captured and abandoned property act, the War Department transferred to the Treasury abandoned lands on which emancipated slaves were employed. Influenced by complaints against the army's labor system, which radicals condemned as de facto serfdom, Secretary Chase tried to put into effect the new Treasury rules evolved in the winter of 1863–64. However, between the dissatisfaction of lessees who had to pay higher wages, the restiveness of freedmen demoralized by the frequent failure of employers to uphold their contracts, and guerrilla raids, Treasury agents were unable to make the new system work.[12]

The decisive consideration was manpower: the Treasury needed laborers for the plantations, but it had to depend on the army's contraband camps to supply them. For its part the army, in need of recruits and responsible for protecting the freedmen and maintaining order, was understandably unwilling to give up the de facto governing function it had acquired over the former slaves. Observing that the new Treasury system was well-intentioned but flawed by "entangling details," Lincoln in February 1864 directed General Thomas to take charge of "the contraband and leasing business."[13] Raising wages somewhat, Thomas reinstated the contract labor system of 1863. The Treasury meanwhile, under a supplementary captured and abandoned property act of July 1864, tried again to secure control of freedmen's affairs, but failed when Lincoln once more sustained the War Department. Only when Congress created the Bureau of Refugees, Freedmen, and Abandoned Lands in the War Department in March 1865 did the jurisdictional struggle over freedmen's policy end.

12. Gerteis, *From Contraband to Freedman*, 138–67.
13. Roy P. Basler et al., eds., *The Collected Works of Abraham Lincoln* (9 vols.; New Brunswick, N.J., 1953–55), VII, 212.

In recent years wartime freedmen's policy has been criticized as being too much like the slave labor system that preceded it, and the sharecropping and tenant farming arrangements of Reconstruction that followed. Several accounts have argued that emancipation did not bring real freedom: freed slaves remained in the South—were indeed kept there by the federal government through systematic policy—as agricultural laborers; were forced to work under exploitative conditions; and continued to live in an economically dependent and socially and politically subordinate relationship to the white majority. White racism appears as the principal explanation of this situation, and slavery is viewed primarily as a form of racial discrimination which, once abolished, was simply replaced by new forms of discrimination. Emancipation undertaken for the wrong reasons—out of military expediency rather than true concern for the well being and rights of the slaves—was bound to produce flawed results. No longer the chattel of individual masters, the freed people became the slaves of society.[14]

Federal officials can justly be criticized for lack of foresight, indifference, and mismanagement of freedmen's affairs.[15] Ultimately, however, the argument that emancipation produced no fundamental change for Negroes is untenable because it fails to take into account the objective benefits that emancipated blacks

14. See Gerteis, *From Contraband to Freedman*; J. Thomas May, "Continuity and Change in the Labor Program of the Union Army and the Freedmen's Bureau," *Civil War History*, XVII (September 1971), 245–54; Messner, "Black Education in Louisiana, 1863–1865"; William F. Messner, "Black Violence and White Response: Louisiana, 1862," *Journal of Sothern History*, XLI (February 1975), 19–38; William L. Barney, *Flawed Victory: A New Perspective on the Civil War* (New York, 1975); William Cohen, "Negro Involuntary Servitude in the South, 1865–1940: A Preliminary Analysis," *Journal of Southern History*, XLII (February 1976), 31–60; John S. Rosenberg, "Toward a New Civil War Revisionism," *American Scholar*, XXXVIII (Spring 1969), 250–72; John S. Rosenberg, "The American Civil War and the Problems of 'Presentism': A Reply to Phillip S. Paludan," *Civil War History*, XXI (September 1975), 242–53; C. Peter Ripley, *Slaves and Freedmen in Civil War Louisiana* (Baton Rouge, 1976).

15. Cf. Nevins, *The War for the Union*, III, 413–44; Wiley, *Southern Negroes*, passim.

received, the radical changes in southern society that resulted from the abolition of slavery, and the wartime exigencies that affected post-emancipation policy. Conceptions of what the Union government might have done measured in twentieth century terms, rather than what it was capable of doing in the context of the 1860s, characterize this unfairly negative view of emancipation.

Recent historians have stressed that the government did not give land to the freedmen, but rather kept the plantations intact and tried to operate them for economic gain. Behind this conclusion is the assumption that land redistribution was a realistic alternative that would have given emancipation real value. It is perhaps regrettable that redistribution was not carried out, but it is not hard to see why it was not. In a general sense the individualistic, self-help ethic of laissez faire capitalism precluded it. More specifically Congress in the Confiscation Act of 1862 decided that property might be taken to help defeat the rebellion, but only temporarily; confiscation was not to continue beyond the lifetime of the offender (to be returned after death to the offender's heirs). In 1864 the House and Senate separately repealed the restriction against permanent divesting of title, but the purpose of the repeal was to prevent rebel lands temporarily occupied by freed slaves from reverting to the rebel owner's family should the owner be killed in battle. The aim was to protect freed slaves in the temporary use of the land, not to give them the land outright. The Captured and Abandoned Property Act of 1863 similarly brought rebel lands under temporary Union control, while the Freedmen's Bureau Act of 1865 gave former slaves the use of abandoned lands as a form of assistance with only a remote possibility of acquiring title.[16]

If land redistribution was unlikely, and if there was good reason to operate plantations for the benefit of the Union, it followed that emancipated slaves would form an agricultural labor force. It followed also that they would work under white

16. James G. Randall, *Constitutional Problems under Lincoln* (revised ed., Urbana, 1951), 317–28; *Cong. Globe*, 38 Cong., 1 Sess. (June 27, 1864).

employers, either on privately leased or government-run plantations. What has impressed many recent historians is the continuation of white control, as though there were no difference between antebellum planters and wartime or postwar freedmen's officials. What impressed contemporaries—including blacks who fled to Union lines in large numbers all through the war—was the difference between the two groups. One of them was committed to slavery, the other to free institutions.

The labor contract, a principal feature of free labor economics and a key part of Union freedmen's policy, has been viewed as a continuation of the antebellum mode of labor organization.[17] If slavery is defined as Negro labor on plantations run by white persons, then it did continue to exist, in a different form, during the war and Reconstruction. To contemporaries, however, slavery meant denial of the slave's ownership of himself, of the right of locomotion and personal liberty, of the fruits of his labor.[18] The motivation of slave labor was the whip; the motivation of contract labor was the same human ambition that propelled free market capitalism. To be sure, there were abuses in the government's freedmen's policy, but even with its flaws it was profoundly different from slavery. The contract labor system changed the motivation of black labor and introduced concern for Negro workers' rights. Radicals who protested the government's freedmen's policy during the war acknowledged the difference from slavery even while discounting its significance. Comparing General Banks's labor policy to an "ideal and perfect system" and finding it profoundly flawed, the Boston *Commonwealth* asked what difference it made that the government's system was better than that of the rebel South.[19] Most people of the time, however, saw vast significance in the difference.

Freedmen's wages were considerably lower than peacetime wages for free blacks. This was a matter to be decided more by

17. Gerteis, *From Contraband to Freedman*, 52.

18. David Brion Davis, *The Problem of Slavery in the Age of Revolution 1770–1823* (Ithaca, 1975), 266–67.

19. Boston *Commonwealth*, December 17, 1864, editorial.

economic realities and wartime necessities, however, than by idealistic aspirations. The capacities and abilities of freed blacks were considered a major question mark.[20] Indeed the first thing the northern public wanted to know was whether emancipated slaves would work for a living.[21] Under the circumstances the market value of freedmen's labor was unknown. Nor was it known how much loyal planters and northern lessees would be willing to pay emancipated slaves.[22] These planters and lessees acquired particular influence in determining post-emancipation policy because, in addition to their economic importance, they formed a potential Unionist constituency.

Because Union authorities were opposed to slavery and committed to free labor, they were in an important sense on the side of the freedmen. White planters, for example, objected to the free labor system in Louisiana on the ground that Negroes would work only under the coercion of slavery. They criticized Banks's policy for failing to control the black population.[23] In fact native whites no longer exercised complete control over blacks, who now enjoyed some of the ordinary civil rights identified with citizenship. They were paid for their work; received physical protection and had recourse in case of injury; were free to move about within the limits imposed by the war; and in many places were educated in army schools. In the view of W. E. B. DuBois, wartime policies toward the freedmen were generally beneficial. Where blacks were treated honestly and assisted in their education, DuBois believed, as in the Sea Islands, North Carolina, Louisiana, and the Mississippi valley, the results were good. No longer machines run for others' profit, blacks now produced for themselves, and their standard of living rose. DuBois concluded that although mismanagement and cruelty existed in freedmen's policy, Negroes accomplished

20. Nevins, *The War for the Union*, III, 438; Samuel Gridley Howe to Charles Sumner, September 17, 1862, Howe Papers, Harvard University Library.
21. *Liberator*, May 22, 1863, speech of Edward L. Pierce.
22. Nevins, *The War for the Union*, III, 430.
23. Gerteis, *From Contraband to Freedman*, 89–90.

their first aim of escaping from the discipline of the planta-tion.[24]

To be sure, emancipated slaves lived under social and eco-nomic conditions that whites largely controlled.[25] This circum-stance, however, does not negate the significance of emancipa-tion. Some kind of social control and organization were necessary to replace the system of slavery.[26] To conclude that Union policy tried to alleviate the upheaval and dislocation of emancipation does not mean, as some historians have sug-gested, that the government tried to maintain antebellum pat-terns of land use and labor organization.[27] On the contrary, contract labor, sharecropping, and lease and purchasing ar-rangements that blacks entered into represented new uses of the land and new modes of labor organization.

It is necessary also to consider the view that Union freed-men's policy kept emancipated blacks in the South out of defer-ence to northern race prejudice. According to this interpreta-tion, black containment was accomplished by enlisting freed slaves in the army, organizing them as a free labor force, and when necessary denying them the right to leave the planta-tions.[28] The containment thesis implies that but for the gov-ernment's restraints on them, southern freedmen would have enjoyed a more substantial liberty based on genuine mobility. The evidence suggests, however, that although blacks moved about in testing their new right of personal liberty, they did not wish to leave the South.[29] The northern public was certainly

24. W. E. B. DuBois, *Black Reconstruction in America 1860–1880* (Cleveland and New York, 1964; orig. publ. 1935), 79.

25. Messner, "Black Violence and White Response: Louisiana, 1862," 36.

26. Willie Lee Rose, " 'Iconoclasm Has Had Its Day': Abolitionists and Freedom in South Carolina," in Martin Duberman, ed., *The Anti-slavery Vanguard: New Essays on the Abolitionists* (Princeton, 1965), 182.

27. Gerteis, *From Contraband to Freedman,* 52.

28. V. Jacque Voegeli, *Free but Not Equal: The Midwest and the Negro during the Civil War* (Chicago, 1967), passim, esp. 95–112.

29. Peter Kolchin, *First Freedom: The Responses of Alabama's Blacks to Emancipation and Reconstruction* (Westport, 1972), 4–7.

interested in this question, and was opposed to any large-scale Negro migration out of the South. But it would be a mistake to regard northern opinion on this score as a crucial factor in the evolution of Union freedmen's policy. Wartime exigencies were the compelling consideration, and provide a sufficient explanation of the government's course of action. Not only was it common sense to employ freed slaves as the administration did, but the blacks had their homes in the South and naturally wished to stay there. Regional conditions, furthermore, which had inhibited free black migration before the war, could be expected to make interregional migration after emancipation unlikely.[30] The immediate issue finally was not whether freed slaves would go North, but whether they would stay South or be colonized. As late as October 1864, a national convention of colored men placed first on its list of demands the right to remain on American soil.[31]

It is fair to ask whether the government could have relocated freed slaves in the North and West, in order to fill labor shortages and relieve the army of the welfare burden emancipation forced it to assume.[32] Perhaps it could have, according to twentieth century theories of social engineering, but not under prevailing nineteenth century governmental theories and racial attitudes. It is by no means clear moreover that opposition to government-supervised freedmen's migration to the North was based mainly on racial prejudice. Committed advocates of Negro rights such as Massachusetts Governor John A. Andrew reasoned that northern settlement would place blacks in a hostile environment where they would be unable to help themselves.[33] Senators Charles Sumner and Henry Wilson of Massachusetts, leading defenders of the freedmen's cause in Congress, objected to plans for government relocation of blacks

30. Ira Berlin, "The Structure of the Free Negro Caste in the Antebellum United States," *Journal of Social History*, IX (Spring 1976), 307–313.
31. New Orleans *Tribune*, October 25, 1864.
32. Voegeli, *Free but Not Equal*, 110, argues in the affirmative.
33. Ibid., 58–59.

because the plans were offered by border state conservatives who were trying to embarrass the Republican party. If Negroes had little inclination to move North, and if proposals for Negro migration out of the South were principally a political tactic,[34] then the argument that the government denied freed slaves meaningful freedom by failing to relocate them in the North is not persuasive.

All who were concerned with freedmen's policy were forced to consider how, in view of the debilitating effects of slavery, former slaves could be expected properly to exercise the rights of civil liberty without supervision. Free republican institutions appeared as a solution to this problem.[35] Northerners believed that in a republican civil order the freedmen would, in the language of the day, fulfill their potential for manhood and citizenship. Wartime policies based on free contractual labor had the purpose of steering emancipated slaves along the path of laissez faire legal equality. Although army officials exercised much control over freedmen's affairs, causing critics like Wendell Phillips to complain that government policy lacked any genuine element of consideration,[36] the contract labor system was intended to help freedmen become self-supporting. To a considerable extent it succeeded.[37]

As Union armies improvised policies in the field, northern political leaders and reformers debated the post-emancipation future of Negroes in the United States. Their discussions gave expression to the laissez faire climate of opinion in which freedmen's legislation, culminating in the Freedmen's Bureau Act of 1865, took place.

Before the war the consequences of emancipation had not been an issue among opponents of slavery. Holding that the slaves would know what to do with their freedom when they got

34. *Liberator*, June 24, 1864, Annual Report of the New England Freedmen's Aid Society.

35. Rose, " 'Iconoclasm Has Had Its Day,' " 202.

36. *National Anti-Slavery Standard*, May 14, 1864, speech of Wendell Phillips.

37. Martha M. Bigelow, "Freedom of the Mississippi Valley, 1862–1865," *Civil War History*, VIII (March 1962), 38–47.

it, abolitionists believed that to consider problems resulting from immediate emancipation implied that the source of such problems was Negro inferiority rather than white prejudice.[38] In effect, therefore, at the start of the war the answer to the question of what should be done with freed Negroes was to leave them alone: simply give them freedom under the same laws that governed the rest of the community.[39]

The abolitionist Lewis Tappan, assuming that colonization would fail, envisioned freed slaves protected against oppression by state laws and kept responsible by local vagrancy laws, but otherwise left free to make their own labor contracts, enjoy the rewards of labor, and receive the benefit of public schools.[40] Republican congressman George W. Julian's advice in January 1862 was to free the slaves, "leave them to the law of their condition . . . and let them have fair play in fighting the battle for life."[41] When it was proposed to appoint guardians to care for very young and old emancipated slaves in the District of Columbia, Senator Lot M. Morrill of Maine objected on the ground that blacks needed rights, not favors. "Just take your feet off these people," Morrill said. "They do not ask your charity . . . they will take care of themselves."[42] Reviewing the administration decision to make freed blacks army laborers and soldiers, the Boston *Commonwealth* expressed doubt that the government could do any more than it had. It was "Eutopian [sic] to expect the emancipation of four million slaves on any theory of philanthropy," the *Commonwealth* declared: the Negro "must do the remainder for himself."[43]

38. *Liberator*, September 11, 1863, essay by James A. Thome; Aileen S. Kraditor, *Means and Ends in American Abolitionism: Garrison and His Critics on Strategy and Tactics, 1834–1850* (New York, 1967), 26–27.

39. *National Anti-Slavery Standard*, January 24, 1863, editorial.

40. Lewis Tappan, *Immediate Emancipation: The Only Wise and Safe Mode* (New York, 1861), in Frank Freidel, ed., *Union Pamphlets of the Civil War 1861–1865* (2 vols.; Cambridge, 1967), I, 102–17.

41. George W. Julian, *Speech in the House of Representatives . . . January 14, 1862* (Washington, 1862), 14.

42. *Cong. Globe.* 37 Cong., 2 Sess., 1477 (April 1, 1862).

43. Boston *Commonwealth*, November 29, 1862, editorial.

As the army organized freedmen's labor systems, many reformers criticized it for controlling the freedmen too closely. Former slaves were not wards or apprentices who needed provost marshals to look after them, argued the *Commonwealth* in December 1864. Blacks were able—provided government lifted its hand from their shoulders—to judge their own interests and make their way in the world.[44] Although some radicals believed that justice for the freedmen should include political rights, Benjamin F. Butler expressed the prevailing view when he said that beyond the protection that legal equality provided, "The Negro is to be left severely alone."[45]

Negroes themselves strongly advocated a laissez faire policy based on equality before the law. Placing civil and political rights uppermost, Negro leaders in 1864–65 urged economic and moral self-help and improvement. Frugality, accumulation of property, self-reliance—the classic bourgeois virtues—formed the substance of their laissez faire appeal, and none expressed it more forcefully than Frederick Douglass. "I have had but one answer from the beginning," Douglass said when the question of the disposition of the freedmen came up: "Do nothing with us! Your doing with us has already played the mischief with us."[46] The black abolitionist Henry Highland Garnet, speaking near the end of the war, said the reform movement would end when the black man "in every respect . . . shall be equal before the law, and shall be left to make his own way in the social walks of life."[47]

The laissez faire approach to freedmen's affairs, however, was not the only one. Observing the actual condition of the freed people, many abolitionists and radicals believed they needed guidance and supervision in adapting to freedom. Thus James Yeatman, a leader in the freedmen's relief movement,

44. Ibid., December 17, 1862, editorial.

45. Ibid., February 11, 1865, speech of B. F. Butler.

46. Philip S. Foner, ed., *The Life and Writings of Frederick Douglass* (4 vols.; New York, 1955), IV, 164.

47. McPherson, *The Negro's Civil War*, 290; August Meier, "Negroes in the First and Second Reconstructions of the South," *Civil War History*, XIII (June 1967), 117–120.

insisted in December 1863 that the government had a duty to exercise "a wholesome guardianship" over emancipated blacks.[48] The *Independent*, a radical religious weekly, held that blacks were children to a considerable extent and needed to be treated accordingly.[49] In part this paternalistic tendency grew out of a humanitarian impulse. Yet it was also based on the belief that all blacks, not just freed slaves, constituted an exceptional class or interest which, like American Indians, required special government action and explicit legal recognition.[50]

The idea of guardianship for freed slaves received backing from the American Freedmen's Inquiry Commission, a government-appointed agency that was representative of the antislavery establishment. Charged with studying post-emancipation problems, the A.F.I.C. advised guardianship for Negroes. Explaining that the apprenticeship system adopted in the West Indies after emancipation was faulty in details rather than general conception, the Commission regarded it as an open question whether or how soon blacks would be able to become self-supporting in view of the racial prejudice and disabilities imposed on them by slavery.[51] As for the length of time guardianship would be needed, some reformers suggested seven years. In advocating the creation of an executive department of freedmen's affairs, however, as they did in 1865, radicals seemed to assume that blacks required indefinite regulation by the federal government.[52]

The attraction of laissez-faire was such that advocates of

48. James E. Yeatman, *A Report on the Conditions of the Freedmen of the Mississippi, presented to the Western Sanitary Commission, December 17, 1863* (St. Louis, 1864), 6, 16.

49. *Independent*, August 20, 1863, editorial.

50. J. W. Phelps to Charles Sumner, December 23, 1864, Sumner Papers, Harvard University Library.

51. American Freedmen's Inquiry Commission, Preliminary Report, June 30, 1863, Thirty-seventh Congress, *Senate Executive Documents*, No. 53.

52. Robert Dale Owen to Charles Sumner, March 24, 1864, Sumner Papers, Harvard University Library; William Whiting, *War Powers under the Constitution of the United States* (43rd ed., Boston, 1871), 464–66.

government paternalism frequently felt compelled to recognize it. While proposing strict government supervision, the A.F.I.C. pointed out that freed slaves must be taught that emancipation meant neither idleness nor gratituous work, but fair labor for fair wages. As soon as possible, urged the reform group, the freed people should be treated as men from whom self-reliance and self-support were demanded.[53] The *Independent* observed that while the freedmen's question would not take care of itself, neither must the government regulate the freed people too closely.[54] Samuel Gridley Howe, a member of the A.F.I.C., further illustrated the conflict between the paternalistic impulse and the laissez faire imperative. Criticizing the army's freedmen's policy in 1863, Howe offered suggestions that added up to a more comprehensive and systematic method of regulating emancipated slaves. Yet the objective of government policy, he wrote, should be to regulate Negro labor by "the ordinary principles of demand and supply" and eliminate administrative machinery."[55] Through logic that other antislavery men regarded as inconsistent, Howe in effect held that government guardianship would teach the freedmen to succeed on their own.

Conflict between paternalistic supervision and laissez faire detachment formed a central theme in wartime legislation concerning emancipated slaves. At the start of the war Congress had no well developed policy on the rights of the ex-slaves, much less the means of securing them. Emancipation measures of 1861–62, for example, inspired as they were by military and political motives, generally contained no provisions for securing and guaranteeing the personal liberty of slaves who were declared free.[56] The only expression of legislative interest in

53. American Freedmen's Inquiry Commission, Preliminary Report, 13, 15, 19.

54. *Independent*, August 20, 1863, editorial.

55. Samuel Gridley Howe to Charles Sumner, June 11, 1863, Howe Papers, Harvard University Library.

56. An exception was an emancipation bill passed by the House in June 1862 which extended to freed slaves the privilege of the writ of habeas corpus against state officers and private persons who might detain them.

freedmen's rights came in the colonization laws, which referred to the settlement of Negroes abroad "with all the rights and privileges of freemen."[57] Gradually, however, an interest in freedmen's and Negroes' rights began to emerge. Congress removed certain racial barriers, as when it repealed the black code of the District of Columbia, admitted witnesses irrespective of color in District of Columbia courts, and eliminated racial restrictions on service in the federal militia in the Militia Act of 1862. By the time treatment of freed slaves in the occupied South became an issue in 1863, blacks, by virtue of army service, were acting and being considered as part of the people of the United States, and as persons, if not yet clearly citizens, under the Constitution.

From 1862 to 1865 Republican Congressmen tried to systematize, improve, and write into law the freedmen's policies devised by Union armies in the occupied South. A paternalistic approach was evident in the earliest measure proposed, for the colonization of freed slaves as apprentices on abandoned plantations in Florida.[58] Another measure, passed by the Senate in 1862, created a board of guardians in South Carolina charged with overseeing the wage labor of freedmen and providing them with food, clothing, shelter, and medical care.[59] After the Emancipation Proclamation, Representative Thomas D. Eliot of Massachusetts proposed a Bureau of Emancipation in the War Department to adjust and determine all questions concerning the general superintendence, disposition, and direction of freed slaves. The Bureau would in Eliot's view govern emancipated blacks so as to protect their rights and interests, and also those of the nation.[60]

The idea of guardianship found succinct expression in Eliot's 1863 bill. Thereafter, however, a laissez faire reaction set in

---

57. *U.S. Statutes at Large*, XII, 592 (Second Confiscation Act).

58. Thirty-seventh Congress, H.R. No. 121, December 9, 1861, introduced by John Gurley.

59. Thirty-seventh Congress, S. No. 201, February 14, 1862.

60. Thirty-seventh Congress, H.R. No. 683, January 19, 1863, introduced by Thomas D. Eliot.

that modulated the paternalistic tendency. Freedmen's bureau bills passed by the House and Senate in 1864 reflected this development. Though the House bill for a Freedmen's Bureau closely followed Eliot's initial proposal, it differed by authorizing freedmen to occupy and cultivate abandoned rebel estates. This provision implied, without actually defining, a right of independent free labor, presumably to be regulated by contract for wages or a share of the crop. In overall effect, however, the House bill ratified the army's labor system, for it instructed Bureau agents to advise, organize, and direct freed slaves' labor, and to adjust their wages and receive returns arising from their use of the land.[61]

The House bill was rejected by the Senate Committee on Slavery and Freedmen in part because it seemed to provide inadequate protection of freedmen's liberty.[62] A substitute measure approved by the Senate placed the Freedmen's Bureau in the Treasury Department, apparently because many Republicans believed Treasury agents were more alert in defense of freedmen's welfare and rights than army officers. While this bill was intended to confirm the policies that the Treasury Department introduced in 1863–64, it gave clearer expression to the idea of laissez faire legal equality than the House bill did. Thus it stated that emancipated slaves were to be protected in their rights, treated as free men with all proper remedies in courts, and subjected to the exercise of no control except in conformity with law. Underscoring the theoretical importance of the labor contract, the Senate bill also announced that freedmen should perform no labor other than under the terms of a voluntary contract. On the other hand, the bill expressly provided for "general superintendence" of emancipated slaves, and assigned bureau agents to act as "advisory guardians" for them.[63]

Republicans who supported the Senate bill saw no conflict

61. Thirty-eighth Congress, H.R. No. 51, December 22, 1863, introduced by Thomas D. Eliot.
62. Charles Sumner to Charles Eliot Norton, May 2, 1864, Charles Eliot Norton Papers, Harvard University Library.
63. Thirty-eighth Congress, H.R. No. 51, May 25, 1864 (Senate substitute).

between government guardianship and vindication of freedmen's liberty and rights. In their view the bill fulfilled the government's responsibility to help emancipated slaves adapt to freedom, while preventing serfdom or apprenticeship in place of slavery.[64] Other antislavery men, however, believed the Senate bill was flawed by excessive government control of the freedmen. "Are they free men or are they not?" asked Republican Senator James Grimes of Iowa. "If they are free men, why not let them stand as free men . . . ?[65]

Republican laissez faire critics of the freedmen's bureau bill, mostly from middlewestern states, had political motives for blocking this favorite project of Massachusetts radical Charles Sumner,[66] and they were assisted by Democrats who were delighted to use a pro-Negro civil liberty argument to attack radicals like Sumner. At the root of the controversy, nevertheless, were conflicting ideas about the proper method of recognizing the freedom and rights of emancipated slaves. Reflecting on the difficulty of the task, freedmen's official John Eaton wrote that while a general confidence existed that Negro liberty would be vindicated, no one could say exactly how the slave was to be transformed into a freeman.[67]

In an attempt to resolve the jurisdictional conflict between the War and Treasury departments, a congressional conference committee in January 1865 proposed to create a Department of Freedmen's Affairs. Although the conference bill contained further refinements intended to assure laissez faire critics that

64. *Cong. Globe*, 38 Cong., 1 Sess., 2799–2800, remarks of Charles Sumner.

65. Ibid., 2972 (June 15, 1864).

66. Massachusetts radicals supported a bill allowing states to fill their draft quotas by enlisting southern Negroes. Mid-west representatives opposed this bill because they felt it gave wealthier states like Massachusetts unfair advantage. Expressing their dissatisfaction, they supported a border state proposal to relocate freed blacks throughout the North. See Richard H. Abbott, "Massachusetts and the Recruitment of Southern Negroes, 1863–1865," *Civil War History*, XIV (September 1968), 198–99, 202–3.

67. John Eaton, *Grant, Lincoln and the Freedmen: Reminiscences of the Civil War* (New York, 1907), 19.

freedmen's rights would be respected, in effect it supported the guardianship idea by regarding the interests of the ex-slaves as sufficiently different from the rest of the population to warrant being placed permanently under a government department. Critics argued that the plan smacked of too much government control; that military protection of the freedmen while the war lasted was all that was needed; and that after the war blacks, able to defend their rights in courts of law, should not be subjected to a special jurisdication different from the rest of the population.[68] The New Orleans *Tribune*, a leading organ of Negro opinion, described the conference committee plan as a "final effort to domination" which presented "the eternal question of tutorage . . . in its most complete and comprehensive form."[69]

As opposition to the new departmental plan took shape, Republican laissez faire critics prepared a bill that was intended temporarily to give the freedmen military protection, humanitarian relief, and occupancy of abandoned lands to help them become self-supporting. The idea behind this bill, which was the work of Ohio radical Robert C. Schenck, was that emancipated slaves should be treated not as a separate class, but as ordinary persons or citizens who for a limited time, because of the misfortunes of war, needed government assistance.[70] The bill expressed this equal rights point of view by abandoning the proposal for a new government department to care for the freed people, and also by including white refugees in the act.

Schenck's bill called for a Freedmen's Bureau in the War Department for the duration of the war that would supervise and manage *subjects* relating to freed slaves (not the freedmen themselves), provide relief assistance, and assign each freedman forty acres of land at 6 percent rent. More than previous bills, this one envisioned the freed blacks of the South as independent farmers rather than contract laborers under the indefinite and

68. New York *Times*, February 7, 1865, letter from F.A.S.

69. New Orleans *Tribune*, January 8, February 7, March 12, 1865.

70. *Cong. Globe*, 38 Cong., 2 Sess., 691 (February 9, 1865), remarks of Robert C. Schenck.

permanent supervisory power of the federal government. References to guardianship found in earlier bills were conspicuously absent from Schenck's plan. The inclusion of white refugees on the other hand resulted from the belief of Republican laissez faire critics that if the government gave assistance to war victims, white persons should receive equal treatment. Explaining that the principle of "no discrimination on account of color" characterized his bill, Schenck headed a second conference committee which reported a bill closely modeled on his own. With the end of the war in sight and the need for systematic legislation on post-emancipation policy becoming imperative, Congress passed this bill and finally created a Freedmen's Bureau. In doing so it looked to laissez faire legal equality as a fundamental principle rather than indefinite guardianship of freed blacks.

Fear that blacks would receive preferential treatment, and a willingness to believe that providing temporary relief would fulfill the government's responsibility toward emancipated slaves, lay back of congressional action on the freedmen's question in 1865. To the modern civil rights sensibility the congressional policy may seem entirely inadequate, indicative of a failure to comprehend the true extent of the difficulties facing blacks in American society. Yet the creation of the Freedmen's Bureau reflected a commitment—too doctrinaire perhaps but certainly characteristic of the times—to legal equality in a laissez faire social context.

The perspective from which most Republicans viewed freedmen's affairs was centered on the destruction of slavery. Because of their hatred of the institution they were averse to any arrangements that seemed to establish indefinite controls over the freedmen. Most Republicans were not as confident as Charles Sumner that mere assurances of freedom and equal treatment, as Sumner's Senate bill provided, were sufficient, especially when a government department would at the same time be charged with superintending the former slaves. A Republican correspondent observed in February 1865 that a majority of antislavery men believed "that if the negro must have a master . . . it makes very little difference whether that master comes from South Carolina or from Massachusetts."[71] The point was that the freedmen must become their own masters, in accordance with more than fifty years of antislavery theory which defined the crucial test of freedom as ownership of one's own person and the absence of physical restraint.[72] Finally, most Republicans compared the present condition of the freedmen with the conditions of slavery rather than with the "ideal and perfect system" that radicals used as a measure of evaluation.[73] In the view of most Republicans the purpose of government policy was to help the freedmen move as far as possible from the dependencies and restraints of slavery.

For many years the standard view of the Freedmen's Bureau was that it intervened actively on behalf of, and exercised controlling influence over, southern blacks in ways that were politically useful to the Republican party. More recently, scholars seeking to understand the failure of Reconstruction have suggested that the Freedmen's Bureau controlled blacks against their best interests by maintaining the South's plantation system and organization of labor.[74] However, while Freedmen's Bureau agents wanted blacks to remain an agricultural labor force, for the obvious reason that jobs were available on plantations, they were committed to the independence of the freedmen in a way that former masters and most white southerners were not. Bureau agents intervened in labor negotiations to help the freedmen become more independent vis-à-vis employers.[75] And the point of the second Freedmen's Bureau Act of 1866 was to strengthen the judicial powers of the Bureau, so freedmen would be able to go to law to secure their rights; it was not to give the Bureau general authority to make rules and regulations for the freed people as a separate class, as Sumner's and Eliot's

71. Cincinnati *Daily Commercial*, February 28, 1865, letter from "Mack."

72. Davis, *The Problem of Slavery in the Age of Revolution*, 266–67.

73. Boston *Commonwealth*, December 17, 1864.

74. See citations above, n. 13; William S. McFeely, *Yankee Stepfather: General O. O. Howard and the Freedmen* (New Haven, 1968).

75. Kolchin, *First Freedom*, 37–38.

bills had proposed and as many radicals urged.[76] To give the freedmen legal recourse to protect themselves, observed the Boston *Commonwealth* in 1866, was to treat them as freemen with equal rights.[77]

American racial attitudes and traditional conceptions of federalism stood as formidable barriers to a successful civil rights policy, and it soon became apparent that the vindication of ordinary civil rights for blacks would require extraordinary efforts by the federal government. The logic of congressional freedmen's policy, however, continued to be that of laissez faire legal—and ultimately political—equality. After defining civil rights and enlarging federal judicial protection in the Freedmen's Bureau Act of 1866, the Civil Rights Act, and the Fourteenth Amendment, Congress extended voting rights to Negroes in the Reconstruction Act of 1867 and the Fifteenth Amendment in 1869. Through these measures, lawmakers hoped, blacks would be able to defend and support themselves without continuing federal intervention. By 1870, then, a national policy that treated emancipated slaves as citizens with ordinary civil rights, rather than as a distinct class requiring federal guardianship, had been written into public law.

Though handed down from above and motivated as much by military and political expediency as hostility to slavery and concern for the welfare of the slaves, emancipation produced social revolution in the South and led to a profound alteration in the status of blacks in the nation as a whole. The pressures of race and politics caused the equal rights principle to be honored more in theory than in practice, but the first years of freedom were nevertheless crucial in determining the long range direction of racial policy in the United States. Equal rights under a single set of laws in each state rather than recognition of blacks as a distinct class or subnational group was to be the standard. These years also marked an important change in the outlook of

76. George R. Bentley, *A History of the Freedmen's Bureau* (Philadelphia, 1955), 134–35; Whiting, *War Powers under the Constitution*, 464.
77. Boston *Commonwealth*, February 3, 1866.

white society toward blacks, for if the imposition of slavery on
Negroes reflected racial attitudes, then the abolition of slavery
did also. The nineteenth century belief in innate Negro inferiority was too deeply entrenched to be dislodged from the white
value system, but emancipation and the subsequent actions of
the freedmen in the war mitigated northern racial prejudice and
caused a shift in public opinion in the Negro's favor.[78]

More important than the question of race, however, was the
concern for democratic principles and institutions. The Republican party defended these principles in defending the Union,
then sought to extend them to the South in resolving post-
emancipation uncertainties concerning the rights of the freedmen. In a relative sense blacks gained the most from this extension of republican institutions, but the consequences transcended
the race question and were beneficial to all Americans. Although
they might not have appreciated it at the time, even white southerners gained from the nationalization of freedom of speech and
of the press and the right of unrestricted interstate transit that
followed the abolition of slavery. By the same token Reconstruction ended in the 1870s not when Negro civil rights were
substantially vindicated—that would require generations to accomplish—but when, amid other considerations, republican
institutions seemed secure enough to permit the relinquishing of
political control over the South.

78. George M. Fredrickson, *The Black Image in the White Mind:
The Debate on Afro-American Character and Destiny, 1817–1914* (New
York, 1971), 167–71.

4

Making the South
Safe for Democracy

*Reconstruction and the
Preservation of State-Rights
Federalism*

LONG BEFORE the war ended, Reconstruction had become a practical political question, and determining the status of the freed slaves was one of its principal aspects. It would be a mistake, however, to view the freedmen's problem, as many recent historians have, exclusively as the central issue in Reconstruction politics and constitutional development.[1] Without denying the relevance of such a perspective to the modern civil rights movement, it is more accurate to say that the organization of state governments in the former Confederacy and their resumption of an active role in the federal system were the most compelling requirements of the time. Together they formed the fundamental issue in Reconstruction.

The question of freedmen's rights was obviously a vital part of this problem, for the constitutional and political legitimacy of

1. Cf. John H. Cox and LaWanda Cox, *Politics, Principle, and Prejudice, 1865–1866: Dilemma of Reconstruction America* (New York, 1963); Eric L. McKitrick, "Reconstruction: Ultraconservative Revolution," in C. Van Woodward, ed., *The Comparative Approach to American History* (New York, 1968), 146–59; Michael Perman, *Reunion Without Compromise: The South and Reconstruction, 1865–1868* (Cambridge, 1973).

reorganized southern governments depended in large measure on the way these governments dealt with the ex-slaves. But the freedmen's question, though it could not of course be ignored, could more readily be left incomplete. The almost universal prejudice against blacks provided constant pressure on Union political leaders to set the Negro question aside, or at least drastically subordinate it to other matters, and the vast and protean shape of the problem of integration meant that it could be resolved at many different levels—in securing equal rights in courts of law, for example—and left unresolved at others. Indeed the problem of equal rights was such that it would be hard to say when it had been satisfactorily resolved. This was not true, however, of the problem of state reorganization. This issue could not be ignored, and the policy alternatives were fewer. Either the states reentered the Union and resumed their proper place in the federal system, or they did not. Except for a few extremists, moreover, no one doubted that they should and would be restored to their traditional position in the constitutional order.[2] The irreducible meaning of Reconstruction therefore was the recognition of legitimate state governments—or, in the language of contemporary political discourse, republican governments—through the seating of senators and representatives in Congress from the former rebel states.

Reconstructing legitimate state governments was not simply a procedural problem; it was also thoroughly substantive. The difficulty lay not in devising an acceptable procedure for bringing the states back into the Union, but in deciding the political and civil character they ought to possess. The concept of republican government, or what a later generation would think of as democracy, provided relevant criteria for answering this question.

Before the war, as noted earlier, slavery threatened republicanism, and the defense of the Union was inextricably bound up with the preservation of free institutions. In the most general

2. For one of a very few exceptions, see Charles Goepp, *The National Club on the Reconstruction of the Union* (New York, 1864).

sense Reconstruction signified an attempt to extend republican institutions into the South, as a logical corollary of the fundamental purpose of the war. Starting with the prohibition of slavery in the Thirteenth Amendment, the ascendant Republican party hoped to inaugurate a republican civil order in the South by establishing freedom of speech and of the press, the right to travel, free public education, and equal citizenship irrespective of race. The dilemma facing national policymakers, however, was that these features of free society could not, consistently with the tenets of republicanism, be unilaterally imposed on the former Confederate states. For whatever else it had meant since the formation of the Constitution, republican government at the very least meant local self-determination and self-government; military government, such as might be necessary to force the South to adopt the free institutions of the North, was its antithesis.[3] Republican government, in other words, rested at bottom on or consisted in voluntary political action by free citizens. It was illogical, paradoxical, and ultimately self-defeating to contemplate the imposition of republican institutions on the defeated southerners.

One of the most perplexing difficulties of the time concerned the meaning of the guarantee clause of the Constitution, the legal instrument by which the free institutions of the North were to be extended into the South. Article IV, section 4 of the Constitution declares that the United States shall guarantee to every state in the Union a republican form of government, and shall protect each state against invasion and domestic violence. Uncertainty existed, however, over whether this provision required the federal government to preserve existing institutions in the states, or authorized it to alter or abolish state institutions. Furthermore the action that the federal government would take in reconstruction would depend not only on the legal authority available through the guarantee clause but also on the perception of actual conditions in the South. Did legitimate local gov-

3. William M. Wiecek, *The Guarantee Clause of the U.S. Constitution* (Ithaca, 1972), 173.

ernment and civil order exist, or were there general disorder and insecurity of life, limb, and property, especially where freedmen and Unionists were concerned? If the former, then for the federal government to impose a new order would be disruptive; if the latter, a policy that sought to create republican institutions was necessary. Finally, given the nature of the conflict as a real war, everyone assumed that its conclusion would somehow result in the subjugation of the defeated. And yet most people acknowledged that conquest had no place in the American constitutional order, which required a large measure of self-government in the states. Even defeated states were expected to be responsible, self-governing units of the polity.

The national government vindicated its authority in the Civil War and exercised an unprecedented degree of power over the states during Reconstruction. In its historical context, however, the more distinctive feature of reconstruction policy was its fidelity to the principle of state-centered republicanism. Much as they desired to secure the results of the war in the aftermath of emancipation, and great though the pressures were in the direction of centralization, Congress was unwilling simply to force the former rebel states under the yoke of northern institutions. From the beginning of the war when they first contemplated the problem of reconstruction, until 1867 when they established a systematic policy for readmitting the seceded states to the Union, Congress acted on the assumption that the people in the states must and would freely and voluntarily reorganize—and reform—their political establishments.

Throughout the 1860s the expectation that the rebellious states sooner or later would willingly assume their responsibilities of local self-government rested on a naive yet remarkably durable belief in white southern Unionism. The earliest discussions of reconstruction, after South Carolina seceded in 1860, assumed that secession was a temporary expedient and that after the extremists had spent themselves politically, southern Unionists would regain control of their state governments and voluntarily return them to the Union. The incoming Republican administration could thus reject war, compromise, and acquiescence in secession for the alternative of peaceful, voluntary reconstruction.[4] This assessment of the situation proved woefully inadequate, but belief in southern Unionism and hope of voluntary restoration persisted as the basis for the initial actions of the federal government on reconstruction.

In July 1861 Lincoln expressed doubt that rebels were a majority in any state except South Carolina and added that he would have no different view of state-federal powers and relations after the rebellion than before it. He also announced that he would recognize Unionists in western Virginia who had formed a loyal government as being the legitimate government of Virginia. Endorsing the voluntary restoration of Virginia, Congress admitted five representatives and senators at the special session in July 1861. Many people believed the action in Virginia showed how, without federal subjugation and with proper regard for states' rights, the Union would be restored. All that was required, declared Senator Timothy Howe of Wisconsin, was to let the instinct of self-government in the loyal people reassert itself in the organization of local government.[5]

The expectations that events in Virginia aroused proved illusory, not only because other states that might have had a substantial Unionist population were unable to restore themselves but also because the West Virginia statehood movement, coming to fruition in 1863, diminished the value of restored Virginia in wartime reconstruction politics. The paradoxical pattern of federal response that was to repeat itself throughout the war and Reconstruction period now became evident. Congress and the administration acknowledged the necessity of more vigorous and extensive use of federal power, yet at the same time clung to the idea that federal action would vivify latent Unionism and enable the people of the rebel states voluntarily to govern themselves in the Union.

In 1862 Lincoln's appointment of military governors in Tennessee, North Carolina, Louisiana, and Arkansas illustrated

4. David M. Potter, *Lincoln and His Party in the Secession Crisis* (New Haven, 1942), 219–48.

5. *Cong. Globe*, 37 Cong., 1 Sess., 380–81 (Aug. 1, 1861).

the pattern. Acting under the "grasp of war" theory, which allowed the government to exercise extraordinary power for military purposes, Lincoln aimed at creating governments-in-exile that might counteract the effect of Confederate rule. Emphasizing speed in the formation of loyal state organizations at the expense of antislavery reform, he instructed military governors in the fall of 1862 to hold elections for representatives to Congress, state legislators, executive officers, and United States senators. Although it was the very absence of spontaneous local Unionism that made these federal efforts necessary, Lincoln persisted in the illusion—or more accurately the legal fiction—of voluntarism. The paradoxical position in which the party's commitment to federalism and voluntary self-government placed the administration was apparent in Lincoln's admonition, even as he took control of reconstruction, that elections for representatives should be the result of a movement of the people rather than Union military authorities. The point, Lincoln explained, was for the people of the occupied South to show their willingness to vote for members of Congress, and to support the Constitution.[6]

Electing members of Congress as a process of reconstruction was nationalist in its implications, yet it also respected states' rights. The election of representatives expressed the popular origins of the Union and the direct relationship that existed between the people of the United States and the national government. Although states had traditionally supervised this national function, state power was not essential to it.[7] At the same time the choice of representatives signified the existence of the states, for only in a legitimate state government could people elect members of Congress. Citizens in the national territories did not enjoy this right. The government's restoration

6. Roy P. Basler, et al., eds., *The Collected Works of Abraham Lincoln* (8 vols. plus index, New Brunswick, N.J., 1953–55), V, 303, 445, 462–63, 504–5.

7. Richard P. Claude, "Constitutional Voting Rights and Early U.S. Supreme Court Doctrine," *Journal of Negro History*, LI (April 1966), 114–24.

policy in 1862 thus blended nationalist with states' rights elements, and stronger federal action with the appearance at least of voluntary local action.

It is impossible to evaluate fully the voluntary character of the elections held in the occupied South in 1862, but the participation of more than 7,600 voters in Louisiana, 1,400 in eastern Virginia, and 1,900 in a district in Tennessee seemed neither inconsiderable nor entirely a matter of legal fiction.[8] Led by conservative Republican Henry L. Dawes of Massachusetts, Congress confirmed the administration's restoration policy by seating representatives from Louisiana in 1863.

Dawes explained the theory behind the congressional action in observing that however reconstruction might begin, whether through a convention of loyal citizens or, as in the case of Louisiana, by the action of the military governor calling an election, the loyal people were entitled to representation. And the government, under its constitutional obligation to guarantee each state a republican form of government, was required to see that they were represented. Congressmen could thus minimize the degree of federal intervention in Louisiana, could indeed regard it as the response to a constitutional command, and emphasize the uncoerced nature of local Unionist activity. The House committee on elections reported that in conducting the election the military governor of Louisiana had followed state law and met no local Unionist resistance. The conclusion followed that the procedure employed in Louisiana enabled the people to exercise the franchise in a "free and untrammeled and unawed" way, so that Congress had only to recognize "the spontaneous voice of these electors. . . ."[9]

Although Congress overwhelmingly voted to readmit Louisiana, several Democrats and Republicans objected to what they regarded as unconstitutional control of local affairs by the mili-

8. *House Reports*, 37 Congress, 3 session, No. 22, No. 23, No. 46; Herman Belz, *Reconstructing the Union: Theory and Policy During the Civil War* (Ithaca, 1969), 107.
9. *Cong. Globe*, 37 Cong., 3 sess., 832–33 (February 9, 1863), remarks of Henry L. Dawes; *House Reports*, 37 Cong., 3 sess., No. 22.

tary. Their political reasons for opposing the admission of Louisiana notwithstanding, the critics called attention to the inherent contradiction in the policy of using national power to encourage voluntary local self-government. In their view military government by definition was unrepublican. Critics also questioned the assumption underlying Louisiana recognition that the states were still in the Union and able to be restored merely through the election of representatives. Against this theory radicals proposed an alternative approach to reconstruction which depended on a different view of the status of the seceded states.

Throughout the 1860s the status of the rebel states was the kind of legalistic question that everyone agreed was theoretical and hardly worth arguing about, but that at the same time evoked strong emotions and was the subject of endless debate. Clearly something quite real was at stake in these discussions, and abstract as the issue seemed, the way it was resolved was a matter of considerable practical consequence.[10] Regarding the war as an insurrection of disloyal citizens against their government, the Lincoln administration in any case viewed the states as indestructible parts of the federal system and still in the Union. At most the government might hold the rebels in the grasp of war, while permitting loyal citizens to reorganize local civil authority and govern themselves. Whether this reorganization should occur through local initiative, as in western Virginia, or with federal supervision, as in Louisiana, the result would be the voluntary restoration of the states to their place in the federal system.

A second approach to the question of rebel state status defined the conflict as a full-scale war under the law of nations and viewed the states as no longer in the Union. The conflict

10. The most obvious point is that the powers legally available to the government depended on how the conflict was defined. If southerners were disloyal citizens, the government could deal with them in one way; if enemies, another. Beyond this practical consideration, the nature of the war and the status of the states had value as a symbolic issue through which lawmakers could identify themselves politically and appeal to public opinion.

may have begun as a struggle against a usurping faction with a Union party in existence in the South, observed legal writer Sidney George Fisher. But, he added, it was soon apparent that the vast majority of southerners supported the Confederacy and that the contest was "in some respects, a foreign war between two contiguous nations."[11] William Whiting, Solicitor in the War Department and the chief publicist of this theory of the war, held that the Confederacy was a belligerent, that all persons in the rebel states were public enemies, and that the seceded states no longer existed.[12] Extreme as this outlook was, it contained elements of undeniable truth which became the basis of the Supreme Court's holding, in the Prize Cases of 1863, that the Union government could treat southerners both as rebels and enemies.

Still another answer to the question of the status of the seceded states lay in the theory and practice of territorial government. Even before the war began many people viewed the seceding states in the light of the territorial model. States that rejected the Union, the argument ran, became federal property or territories subject to congressional legislative power.[13] In the first year of the war, after voluntary restoration had clearly failed, this outlook formed the basis for a legislative theory of reconstruction which held that while secession was illegal and ineffective as far as taking states out of the Union was concerned, lawful state governments had ceased to exist in the rebel states. In law and in fact they became unorganized territory. Since territorial status was a recognized condition under the Constitution, however, this southern territory was of course still part of the Union. Accordingly territorial reconstruction theorists still recognized, albeit in an ironic way, the idea of local

11. Sidney George Fisher, *The Trial of the Constitution* (Philadelphia, 1863), 363.
12. William Whiting, *War Powers Under the Constitution of the United States*, 43rd ed. (Boston, 1871), 235–46.
13. Cf. New York *Tribune*, February 5, 1861, correspondence from "G"; New York *Evening Post*, February 2, 1861, editorial; Trenton *Daily Gazette and Republican*, January 18, 1861; *Cong. Globe*, 36 Cong., 2 Sess., 138 (December 19, 1860), remarks of Andrew Johnson.

autonomy. The federal government could not remand states to territories, said Representative Fernando C. Beaman of Michigan; only the people in the states could do that by voluntarily abandoning their proper constitutional responsibilities.[14]

If the sole purpose of the war was to restore the federal Union to the status quo ante bellum, military power alone would be sufficient. If changes in state laws and constitutions should become necessary, however, then the government would need some additional source of power. This of course was the situation that developed after the Emancipation Proclamation went into effect. Many people concluded that the Lincoln administration's theory of the war as an insurrection, with its corollary of state indestructibility, was inadequate because it did not provide authority for requiring the changes in state constitutions that now seemed necessary. In contrast the theory of international war, based on the idea that southerners were enemies and the states conquered alien provinces, supplied ample authority for this purpose. So too did the theory of territorialization, which called for the appointment of governors and legislators empowered to deal with all rightful subjects of legislation under the Constitution. Stated in this way, as it was in several congressional reconstruction bills, the territorial theory permitted the abolition of slavery.

Although the conquered provinces and territorial theories were identified with antislavery purposes, and hence politically radical, they were moderate constitutionally because they did not propose to abolish federalism and states' rights. Each provided a way of controlling local affairs and altering municipal institutions, yet each also assumed that local action by southerners would lead to the restoration of constitutional state organizations. Cautioning against a complete restoration of antebellum federalism that would give the states plenary power over personal liberty, War Department counsel William Whiting in 1863 urged alterations in state constitutions. It was necessary to insist on such changes, however, precisely because of the

14. Ibid., 37 Cong., 2 Sess., 1551–54 (April 4, 1862).

universal assumption that the war did not permanently enlarge federal power at the expense of the states, and that the states would return to the Union with their prewar powers intact except where slavery was concerned.[15] Maintaining the perspective of voluntary self-government, Whiting envisioned reconstruction proceeding through the action of the people forming state governments based on antislavery constitutions. For the time being military government must prevail in the occupied South, but ultimate responsibility for establishing republican government belonged to the loyal people in the states.[16]

Although it was small solace to conservatives, advocates of territorialization also expected reconstruction to occur through the voluntary efforts of local Unionists. Several bills introduced into Congress in 1861–63 proposed to establish territorial governments in occupied states, but these were provisional organizations the primary purpose of which was to maintain order. Some of the reconstruction bills stated that territorial governments would continue until the loyal people created a new state government and applied for admission to the Union as a state.[17] Others simply declared that provisional government would continue until the old state governments were reestablished under the Constitution.[18] None of the bills prescribed procedures to be followed in reestablishing state governments.

The territorial approach to reconstruction differed sharply in political character from the administration's policy of military government. Conservative Unionists thought that territorialization recognized the effectiveness of secession in altering the legal condition of the states, and it obviously represented a greater exercise of federal authority than the restoration of loyal Virginia required in 1861. Nevertheless, the territorial approach

15. Michael Les Benedict, "Preserving the Constitution: The Conservative Basis of Radical Reconstruction," *Journal of American History*, LXI (June 1974), 69.

16. Whiting, *War Powers*, 230–34, 248–49.

17. Thirty-seventh Congress, H.R. No. 356, H.R. No. 236, File of Printed Bills of the U.S. Congress, Library of Congress.

18. Thirty-seventh Congress, S. No. 132, S. No. 200, File of Printed Bills of the U.S. Congress, Library of Congress.

imposed no more federal power than the policy of military government, and it acknowledged local self-determination. Indeed the reconstruction bills of 1862 were an adaptation of the American tradition of territorial government. Since 1789 the forming of new states had been a national responsibility, discharged by Congress through its power to legislate for the territories and authorize their admission into the Union as states. At the same time, however, national controls lay lightly on the people in the territories, who in practical effect possessed the power to form new state polities. Long before Stephen Douglas appropriated the term, they exercised popular sovereignty in shaping institutions of local government.[19]

Throughout the war planners of Congressional reconstruction acknowledged this element of local autonomy. Insisting that disloyal persons be excluded from reconstruction, Fernando Beaman said the lesson must be taught that the people of a state could not abolish their government and reconstruct it at pleasure. They could, however, reconstruct it after a period of provisional government under national control, which would last as long as the loyal were too few to act authoritatively.[20] Although by 1863 the necessity of federal supervision was taken for granted, the Philadelphia *Press* reported that most Unionists thought the people of the states should determine questions concerning federal-state relations.[21] Employing the territorial analogy, Alpheus Crosby in 1865 said the government should allow southerners to legislate locally, under supervision, until they formed new governments and reentered the Union as equal states.[22] Although some Republicans accepted a large degree of local responsibility in the hope that the freedmen might vote, their commitment to local autonomy and

19. George M. Dennison, "An Empire of Liberty: Congressional Attitudes Toward Popular Sovereignty in the Territories, 1787–1867," *The Maryland Historian*, VI (Spring, 1975), 19–41.

20. *Cong. Globe*, 37 Cong., 2 Sess., 1553 (April 4, 1862).

21. Philadelphia *Press*, August 10, 1863, letter from "Occasional."

22. Alpheus Crosby, *The Present Position of the Seceded States and the Rights and Duties of the General Government in Respect to Them* (Boston, 1865), 5–14.

voluntarism generally antedated the decisions on Negro suffrage. Indeed commitment to federalism was a reason for giving the freedmen political rights, against the judgment of many Republicans who had doubts about the competence of blacks in the political sphere.

Although it anticipated the restoration of the states and allowed for local political action, territorial reconstruction was unacceptably radical to most members of Congress because it conceded that the seceded states no longer existed as states in the Union. The situation demanded a constitutional course that would regard the rebel states as still in the Union and allow for voluntary reorganization of local authority, yet that would also provide sufficient national power to guarantee safe restoration of the states to their place in the federal system. The guarantee of republican government clause supplied the more moderate constitutional basis that Union lawmakers needed.

The original purpose of the guarantee clause, which declares that the United States shall guarantee to each state in the Union a republican form of government, was to preserve existing institutions against revolution. In the antebellum period antislavery reformers, offering a different interpretation, viewed it as a command to the states to protect civil liberty and as a source of authority by which the federal government might initiate changes in the states to promote that end.[23] At the start of the war Lincoln invoked the clause as justification for the northern military effort, and argued that by resisting secession the government was fulfilling its obligation to guarantee the states republican government.[24] He thus used it in the traditional sense of maintaining existing state governments. From 1863 to 1867, however, Republican lawmakers employed the guarantee clause as an instrument of change. The clause became a reconstruction device providing temporary federal control that would be civil rather than military—the first basic requirement of republicanism—and that would permit the people of the states

23. Wiecek, *The Guarantee Clause of the U.S. Constitution*, 156–65.
24. Basler, ed., *Collected Works of Lincoln*, IV, 440.

voluntarily to exercise a degree of local self-government—the second fundamental element in a republican order.

Guarantee clause theorists rejected the territorial and conquered provinces approaches to reconstruction because these two points of view considered the states destroyed. Under the guarantee clause on the contrary the states still existed, and their existence constituted a limitation on the national authority. Yet clearly secession and war had caused changes in the states. Guarantee clause theorists described the change by saying that the states now existed in a disorganized condition. They lacked legitimate political establishments, or republican governments as required by the Constitution. In consequence the states came under federal jurisdiction and properly became the object of legislative and executive efforts to guarantee them a republican government. Congress and the President could not, however, impose centralized rule on the occupied South. Henry Winter Davis of Maryland, the leading advocate of guarantee clause reconstruction, stated in 1862 that an essential feature of federal enforcement of the guarantee was participation by loyal citizens in reestablishing a government. Davis strongly opposed military subjugation of the South.[25] Republican Senator Ira Harris of New York similarly reasoned that under the guarantee clause the rebellious states were still in the Union and subject to federal legislative power, but only until the loyal citizens were numerous enough to reorganize a state government.[26]

Although in the last eighteen months of the war Republicans adopted reconstruction measures that enlarged the role of the federal government, they continued to hold that southern communities should voluntarily participate in restoring local government. Only marginally successful in restoring states through congressional elections, Lincoln in December 1863 announced a general policy inviting loyal white southern minorities to form new state governments. The Proclamation of

25. Henry Winter Davis to Samuel Francis DuPont, July 11, 1862; Davis to Mrs. S. F. DuPont, October 20, 1862, S. F. DuPont Papers, Eleutherian Mills Historical Library, Greenville, Delaware.

26. *Cong. Globe*, 37 Cong., 2 Sess., 3141–42 (July 7, 1862).

Amnesty and Reconstruction denied pardon to high-ranking confederate officers and required citizens to swear an oath to uphold the Constitution and support the Emancipation Proclamation and other measures dealing with slavery. In this way, Lincoln explained, the country could assure the existence of republican governments. These were the only restrictions on southern Unionists, however, who were otherwise on their own to organize politically.

Obviously one of the most important aspects of local self-government concerned the freedmen, and Lincoln's policy, though insisting on emancipation, in effect allowed the states to determine the status and rights of the former slaves. The executive branch would be agreeable, Lincoln said, to state policies which recognized the permanent freedom of emancipated slaves, provided for their education, and were consistent with their condition as a laboring, landless, and homeless class.[27] Responding to the President's announcement, the radical *New Era* observed that Lincoln's intentions in the matter of reconstruction were less important than the interpretation southerners would make of the invitation thus given them to shape postemancipation policy. Local autonomy was the key to executive policy, and southerners at once appreciated this fact. Some Confederates, arguing that the action of the states themselves had already destroyed slavery, advised repeal of the secession ordinances so that the states could take advantage of the opportunity that Lincoln gave them to secure control of freedmen's labor.[28]

Presidential reconstruction proceeded in Louisiana, where under military supervision moderate Unionists elected a state government and wrote a new constitution in 1864. Sharp controversy between radical and moderate Unionists subsequently led to the charge that army domination of the reconstruction process made the new state government illegitimate. Radical dissatisfaction with General Nathaniel P. Banks's free labor

27. Basler, ed., *Collected Works of Lincoln*, VII, 55.
28. *The New Era*, quoted in *National Principia*, May 5, 1864.

system reinforced this conclusion. In fact, however, the formation of a loyal government in Louisiana rested on considerable local participation, which probably reflected as much voluntary local action as could be expected under the circumstances.

Facing battlefield frustrations and seeking to promote southern Unionism, Lincoln in the latter part of 1864 wavered in his publicly announced commitment to immediate and unconditional abolition. At the peace conference held in Hampton Roads, Virginia in February 1865, he spoke with Confederate leaders about possible compensation for the loss of slave property and prospective ratification of the Thirteenth Amendment. Still trying to encourage voluntary local responsibility, Lincoln a few months later considered recognizing the rebel legislature of Virginia as the legitimate state government, and in his final public address he argued for acceptance of the reorganized Louisiana government. As always, his objective was to support the efforts of white southern Unionists to establish a state government and return to the Union.[29]

Congress approved two reconstruction plans during and after the war—the Wade-Davis bill of 1864 and the Military Reconstruction Act of 1867. These measures insisted on greater federal supervision, imposed more stringent demands, and offered less scope for local initiative than presidential reconstruction policies did. Although not vindictive and draconian devices, they expressed the determination of Republican lawmakers to uphold and extend national authority against the claims of state sovereignty. At the same time, however, the congressional reconstruction plans maintained regard for states' rights, in contradistinction to state sovereignty, and in their own way incorporated the view that successful restoration of the Union required voluntary local action that would reciprocally strengthen both state and federal authority. The new nation so enthusiastically heralded in Unionist oratory would still be a federal Union of republican state governments.

29. Ludwell H. Johnson, "Lincoln's Solution to the Problem of Peace Terms, 1864–1865," *Journal of Southern History*, XXXIV (November 1968), 576–86.

Republicans in the secession crisis had defended federal authority against the charge of unconstitutional coercion of states, and it was a natural extension to assert national power as the central feature of congressional reconstruction. Expressing its persistent interest in reconstruction as well as reacting to the administration's restoration policy in Louisiana, Congress passed the Wade-Davis bill in July 1864. Although generally similar to presidential policy in calling for provisional governments, the bill differed conspicuously in prescribing the course southerners must follow in reorganizing their state governments. After Union authorities enrolled the adult white male population and a majority swore an oath to support the Constitution, elections were to be held for delegates to a constitutional convention. The bill required new state constitutions to abolish slavery, exclude Confederate civil and military officers from voting for or being a member of the state legislature or governor, and prohibit payment of Confederate debts. Only persons who could profess past loyalty could vote for delegates to the convention or participate in the referendum to ratify the new constitution. If the people approved the constitution, the President with the assent of Congress would recognize the state. Properly authorized, the new state government could then hold elections for United States senators and representatives.[30]

Plainly the congressional plan imposed conditions that struck at the idea of voluntary reconstruction. In the eyes of its supporters it asserted the all-important principle that the national legislature should supervise state-making and the formation of republican government, and stood for the triumph of established constitutional authority over unorganized, revolutionary popular action. According to Maryland Representative Henry Winter Davis, its principal author, the 1864 reconstruction bill embodied the idea that every change of government should be carried out under the supervisory authority of an existing legislative body with responsibility to define the rights

30. Thirty-eighth Congress, H.R. No. 244, U.S. Congress, File of Printed Bills, Library of Congress.

of voters and protect the integrity of the electoral process. The "great political law of America," Davis declared in March 1864, was that "somewhere in the United States there is always a permanent, organized legal authority which shall guide the tottering footsteps of those who seek to restore governments which are disorganized or broken down."

Arguing that the Supreme Court had established this principle in the case of Luther v. Borden fifteen years earlier, Davis rejected what he called semirevolutionary attempts to count heads and declare the enumerated persons the people of the state.[31] Under its obligation to guarantee each state a republican government, Congress must intervene and control the people under the forms of law (rather than by military force) until they could organize a state government for themselves.[32] Wendell Phillips agreed that according to the theory of American institutions the people could not create a state government without the authorization of some recognized legislative body. Calling Lincoln's policy of military governments unconstitutional because it ignored this fact, Phillips insisted that for the time being Congress was the only effective governing authority in the occupied South.[33]

Congressional supervision of political change in the seceded states challenged both executive control of reconstruction and self-reconstruction by southern Unionists. In view of Lincoln's attempt to systematize policy, the former aspect assumed greater importance than the latter in 1864.

Most Congressmen regarded Lincoln's Proclamation of

31. In Luther v. Borden (1849) the Supreme Court was asked to determine which of two competing governments in Rhode Island, one of them led by insurrectionary Thomas Wilson Dorr and the other the existing state government, was the legitimate, republican government. The Court, declining to decide, said the question was for Congress to determine in the exercise of its power to guarantee each state in the Union a republican form of government. See George M. Dennison, *The Dorr War: Republicanism on Trial, 1831–1861* (Lexington, 1976).

32. Henry Winter Davis, *Speeches and Addresses* (New York, 1867), 370–83, 272–73.

33. *National Anti-Slavery Standard*, May 17, 1862, speech of Wendell Phillips.

Amnesty and Reconstruction as a useful but by no means conclusive step in formulating a national reconstruction policy.
However one viewed the status of the seceded states, none could
deny that the war had interrupted their relationship to the
Union and deprived them of legitimate republican government.
Under the circumstances the need for civil law was evident, yet
under the separation of powers doctrine law could not emanate
from the executive. Only Congress, with or without presidential
approval, could make law. As early as 1862 therefore many
Republicans argued for a uniform reconstruction law in the
occupied South.[34] Two years later legislation seemed all the
more urgent, even among conservative Unionists who on most
other issues supported executive war powers.[35] The point of
the Wade-Davis bill thus was not to exclude the executive, who
was in fact given a large role in the reorganization process, but
to assure that reconstruction would involve both Congress and
the executive rather than the executive alone. Above all, Congress intended to make state reorganization a process regulated
by law rather than by executive proclamation.[36] Furthermore,
the congressional plan of reconstruction looked to the courts
and the judicial process rather than to the army as a means of
protecting the liberty and rights of emancipated slaves.[37]

Congress was also intent, however, on limiting local sovereignty and asserting national legislative control over state-
making. The admission of West Virginia in 1863 and a series of
statehood bills in 1864 further illuminated this concern.

Although the formation of West Virginia rested in substantial measure on local sentiment, in important respects this state
was the creation of the federal government. Federal troops

34. Cincinnati *Gazette*, July 12, 1862, letter from special correspondent.
35. *National Anti-Slavery Standard*, January 30, 1864, Washington
correspondence.
36. M. L. Benedict, *A Compromise of Principle: Congressional Republicans and Reconstruction, 1863–1869* (New York, 1974), 75.
37. Harold M. Hyman, *A More Perfect Union: The Impact of the
Civil War and Reconstruction on the Constitution* (New York, 1973),
267–68.

made the statehood movement possible, and federal officials manipulated the undertaking to compensate for the lack of voluntary Unionist action in several counties.[38] Moreover, when the new state applied for admission, Congress imposed conditions that signified legislative control of state-making. The West Virginia statehood bill required the people of the state to vote on an amendment to the constitution providing for the gradual abolition of slavery; only upon approval of this amendment could the state enter the Union.[39] According to Davis, Congress thus repudiated the idea that it could impose no conditions on the admission of a state.[40] In 1864 enabling acts for Nevada, Colorado, and Nebraska territories, which required state constitutional conventions to prohibit slavery and form republican governments in accordance with the Declaration of Independence, also established national legislative control over local political action. Conservatives objected to imposing conditions in this way, but most Congressmen saw it as a necessary repudiation of state sovereignty.[41]

Although these measures sought to establish greater federal control over state governments,[42] Republican lawmakers were primarily concerned with redressing the imbalance in federal-state relations that slave power aggressions in the 1850s, based on the theory of state sovereignty, had caused. Republicans were not, in other words, trying to weaken or destroy states' rights. Insisting on congressional regulation of political changes in the seceded states was not inconsistent with recognizing the

38. Richard O. Curry, "The Virginia Background for the History of the Civil War and Reconstruction Era in West Virginia: An Analytical Commentary," *West Virginia History*, XX (July 1959), 215–46.

39. James G. Randall, *Constitutional Problems Under Lincoln*, rev. ed. (Urbana, 1951), 460–61.

40. Davis, *Speeches and Addresses*, 452.

41. *Cong. Glob*, 38 Cong. 1 Sess., 787–88 (February 24, 1864), remarks of Garrett Davis, 1166 (March 17, 1864), remarks of S. S. Cox; Ibid., 39 Cong., 1 Sess., 2372–73 (May 3, 1866), remarks of James M. Ashley.

42. Cf. George M. Dennison, "An Empire of Liberty: Congressional Attitudes Toward Popular Sovereignty in the Territories, 1787–1867," loc. cit., 32.

continued existence of the states and a significant degree of political action therein. In a sense of course any action taken by the people of a state in the wake of military occupation would be coerced. Yet given the persistent belief in southern Unionism, references to voluntary political action in reconstruction legislation expressed respect for the states' rights side of federalism. The Wade-Davis bill thus gave white southerners with a record of wartime loyalty the opportunity to make a new government, and all who swore a prospective oath to the Union the choice of supporting or opposing the new state constitution and government. The bill also held out the possibility that the new state government might be rejected, in which case the provisional government would continue. Because of their commitment to the extensive local autonomy of federalism, Republicans wanted to be sure that the restoration of local government rested on action that was as genuinely voluntary as circumstances allowed.

The Wade-Davis bill also regarded the seceded states as still in the Union. It did not, significantly, treat them as territories, but as states lacking organized republican governments. As derived from the guarantee clause, the power of Congress over reconstruction was less extensive than that which it enjoyed over national territory. Accordingly the Wade-Davis bill required the executive to enforce pre-existing state laws and authorized him to appoint such state officers as he saw fit. Moreover the bill did not exclude those who had participated in presidential reconstruction.[43] Embodying the view that only the people of the states could form new governments, it was essentially an enabling act.[44]

To be sure, the idea that reconstruction should be voluntary was more or less fictional. The point, however, is that it was a legal fiction made necessary by and indicative of the Republican commitment to federalism. Because everyone assumed that the seceded states would soon recover their powers of local gov-

43. Benedict, *A Compromise of Principle*, 81.
44. Ibid., 123.

ernment, it was necessary, if liberty and Union were to prevail, to insist on changes as in the Wade-Davis bill.[45] Congressmen employed the legal fiction of voluntarism because in their attachment to federalism they believed that new state governments, to be legitimate, must rest on the authority and volunatry consent of the people in the states.[46] To refer to voluntary participation as a legal fiction moreover does not mean that no actual spontaneous Unionist action was present. The formation of West Virginia, for example, though it involved federal manipulation and control, also offered evidence of local Unionist political action.[47]

For all their nationalism Republicans continued to think federally, and their most characteristic thought in this respect was that the states were still the principal centers of republicanism. Republicans saw a need to vindicate national power against state sovereignty but not states' rights. On the contrary, states' rights and limited national sovereignty—the essential features of federalism—were complementary, so that enhancement of national power would mean enhancement of state power. The great test for the nation, Union publicist William M. Grosvenor wrote in 1864, was to construct governments for the rebellious states that were a source of strength rather than a burden to the nation.[48] Abolitionist General John W. Phelps stressed the same point, arguing that reconstruction should strengthen and improve state governments in the South, where previously only the outward form of republicanism had ex-

45. *Commonwealth*, September 4, 1863, editorial.

46. Benedict, *A Compromise of Principle*, 123.

47. The administration actually opposed separation and statehood, desiring the restored Virginia government to be as strong as possible. Yet Lincoln was unable to stop the statehood movement. Though Congress favored statehood, antislavery western Virginians played a key role in getting Congress to insist on the terms of admission. Cf. Dallas S. Shaffer, "Lincoln and the 'Vast Question' of West Virginia," *West Virginia History*, XXXII (January 1971), 86–100.

48. Grosvenor to Charles Sumner, December 29, 1864, Sumner Papers, Harvard University Library.

isted.[49] The Republican journalist Charles G. Leland, declaring that the country needed "States Rights according to the Constitution" rather than "disintegrative States Rights" [i.e., state sovereignty], saw the war as a struggle for "federal unity (or republicanism). . . ."[50] Summarizing the complementary relationship between the states and the federal government, the *Independent* observed that northerners, in contrast to southerners, combined a love of states' rights with a strong feeling of nationality.[51]

State-centered republicanism was not a static concept, however, and as emancipation proceeded new ideas about the criteria for republican legitimacy evolved. How to revive state governments in accordance with these changing ideas was of course the central issue in Reconstruction. Grosvenor, Phelps, Charles Sumner, and other radicals argued for a period of outright military rule over the South, on the assumption that the seceded states were too weak as republican commonwealths to control themselves or to be trusted with the regulation of freedmen's affairs. Such an approach was unacceptable, however, since exclusive federal control would deny the element of local participation that distinguished republican government. Republicanism may have been an amorphous concept, but at the very least it meant civil rather than military government, resting on internal consent rather than external coercion.[52] As though in recognition of this basic truth and the corollary notion that local participation must in some sense form part of any reconstruction settlement, Republicans were, in differing degrees, prepared to accept political action by white southerners.

Thus Lincoln promised to accept reorganized loyal governments, and the Wade-Davis bill, though imposing certain condi-

49. Phelps to Charles Sumner, December 21, 1864, Sumner Papers, Harvard University Library.
50. Charles Godfrey Leland, *Centralization or 'States Rights'?* (New York, n.d. [1863], 6–7.
51. *Independent*, August 14, 1862, editorial.
52. Wiecek, *The Guarantee Clause of the U.S. Constitution*, 173.

tions, made readmission contingent on voluntary approval of new constitutions by the people of the states. In the winter of 1864–65 the tendency to accept local action by white southerners as legitimate also appeared in a compromise reconstruction plan introduced by radical Republican James M. Ashley of Ohio, which proposed to recognize the local organizations formed under executive authority in Louisiana, Tennessee, and Arkansas, in return for administration approval of Negro suffrage. A more extreme illustration of the tendency was Ashley's endorsement in February 1865 of a plan to recognize the existing governments in the rebel states as legitimate if they would surrender unconditionally and approve the Thirteenth Amendment.[53] One can see here the essential idea that later characterized moderate reconstruction proposals, namely, that the existing governments in the South be accepted on condition that they assume fundamental obligations in the exercise of states' rights.

That proposals for recognizing the rebel governments were even broached was an indication of the need that existed, despite the official theory of the war as an insurrection of individuals against the government, to reach a peace settlement with the Confederacy. Eric McKitrick has argued persuasively that after Appomattox northerners insisted on certain symbolic requirements going beyond the battlefield verdict.[54] Above all they wanted to guarantee equality before the law for freed slaves, protect Unionists in the South, and repudiate secession. To secure these conditions, however, it was necessary to give southerners some room for action, some genuine range of choice out of which voluntary participation in a settlement could come. Necessarily the coercion of arms conditioned the entire reconstruction process, but military conquest and subjugation were in the long run inadequate for the task at hand. At some point the people in the states must exercise the power of local autonomy—if, that is, the federal system were to be re-

53. Belz, *Reconstructing the Union*, 263–64.
54. Eric L. McKitrick, *Andrew Johnson and Reconstruction* (Chicago, 1960), 21–41.

stored. Since virtually all Republicans, including the most radical, anticipated just this outcome, there was considerable pressure to include southerners in some way in the reorganization process. Given the commitment to federalism, it was imperative that voluntary action at the local level—by the existing white ruling groups if the moderates had their way, by untainted Unionists and the freedmen if the radicals had theirs—demonstrate acceptance of the terms of reunion.

The assassination of Lincoln placed in the White House a War Democrat from Tennessee who proved more than willing to support voluntary action at the local level. The first phase of Andrew Johnson's reconstruction policy required the seceded states to ratify the Thirteenth Amendment, repudiate the Confederate debt, and repeal the ordinances of secession. At the same time, liberally conferring amnesty on former rebels, Johnson gave local populations broad latitude in organizing themselves politically. He invited them to hold conventions to revise their state constitutions, exercise all the powers needed to form republican governments, and restore their states to the Union.[55] Conventions met in the latter part of 1865, and by the end of the year new state governments were operating in all but one of the former rebel states. Secretary of State William H. Seward described the constitutional theory by which presidential reconstruction thus became autonomous local reconstruction. The Union government could withhold amnesty and maintain military control of the former Confederate region, Seward wrote in 1865, but according to the Constitution the people in the states must reorganize state and local authority.[56]

Although most Republicans accepted the legitimacy of President Johnson's policy, they thought it far from conclusive, and several considerations made them unwilling to readmit the restored states to Congress in December 1865. It was unsettling, to say the least, that many former rebels were among the newly elected southern representatives and senators applying for seats

55. Ibid., 49–50.
56. Perman, *Reunion Without Compromise*, 3–4.

in Congress. The fact that Johnson pardoned several ex-confederates after it appeared they would win political office made Republicans doubt that genuine repentance had entered into the amnesty process. Republicans still insisted moreover on substituting national law for executive proclamation as the basis of state restoration. This motive had been part of the reason for passing the Wade-Davis bill, and it played an even larger role in the congressional response to Johnson's policy in 1865. The southern states furthermore had begun to enact laws defining the status and rights and regulating in many respects the lives of the freed people. These laws, known to history as the Black Codes, were the product of the local political organizations that republican theory and practice required to have at hand. Yet these laws created a quasi-slavery or serfdom which was offensive to liberal, humanitarian sentiment, and which also provoked concern for state-centered federalism. In the Republican view the nation consisted of states, and evils in one state or group of states did injury to all the states.[57] Thus a desire to preserve the integrity of the states, and thereby the nation, led Congress to exclude southern delegates and form a Joint Committee on Reconstruction in December 1865.

Though blocking the progress of Johnsonian reconstruction, Congressional Republicans did not abandon the idea that the defeated southerners themselves, perhaps augmented by numbers of freedmen, should participate in the restoration of constitutional federalism.[58] In 1866 moderate Republicans based their reconstruction program on this premise. Reacting against the Black Codes, they extended the life of the Freedman's Bureau. More important, in the Civil Rights Act and the Fourteenth Amendment they established national citizenship and derivative civil rights of Negroes, with the understanding that these rights would be defined by state law and custom. Believing that reconciliation must be part of any reconstruction settlement, moderates were willing to accept the South's political

57. Hyman, *A More Perfect Union*, 296–300.
58. Ibid., 301.

leaders of 1865 provided those leaders accepted the civil rights policy of Congress. To complete the reconstruction process therefore, moderates supported legislation admitting the former rebel states to Congress if they would ratify the Fourteenth Amendment and alter their laws in accordance with it.[59]

The willingness of moderate Republicans to accept and encourage voluntary political action in the states was also evident in the question of suffrage for former rebels. At first inclined to disfranchise from national elections all who had voluntarily participated in the rebellion, moderates finally decided in the Fourteenth Amendment to disqualify only voluntary rebels from officeholding. As a result all adult white males—including former rebels—could vote in national and state elections.[60] The bias of traditional federalism in favor of local political action and self-determination was manifesting itself.

Radicals favored local political action of a different sort. Unwilling to trust the South's present leaders, they proposed to create territorial governments by means of which, during an indefinite period of time, voting populations purged of rebels and strengthened by the addition of freedmen could form republican governments capable of restoring the states to the Union. Radicals thus desired to use federal power to abolish the state governments chosen in 1865. Yet no more than the moderates did they intend to impose a dictated peace on the South. They envisioned instead the growth of a new republican political order in the South that would voluntarily carry the states back into the Union. Because they expected the states to possess substantially the same powers as before the war, except in regard to personal liberty and civil rights, radicals were determined to postpone reconstruction until a more satisfactory basis for reconciliation existed.

The radicals successfully blocked the moderate bill to readmit the seceded states if they would ratify the Fourteenth Amendment. Nevertheless, when Tennessee ratified and was

59. Benedict, *A Compromise of Principle*, 169.
60. Ibid., 183–85.

readmitted in July 1866 it became clear that other states could
return to the Union in the same way. In effect therefore congressional policy gave the ruling groups in the South the choice
of accepting or rejecting the settlement signified by the Civil
Rights Act and the Fourteenth Amendment.

The states of course chose to reject the settlement offered,
so that when Congress met in December 1866 the problem of
restoring the Union remained. Moreover radical and moderate
views continued to be sharply opposed. The radicals wanted to
declare the existing state governments valid for municipal purposes only, and proceed to call constitutional conventions to
effect wholesale political change in the states. Moderates, believing that stable reunification required the participation and
consent of the South's recognized leaders, still hoped to deal
with the Johnson governments chosen in 1865. The moderate
outlook rested not only on an instinctive aversion to political
upheaval but also on the assumption that if the states were still
in the Union they must take responsibility for governing themselves. It was significant in any case that the central question in
1866–67 was how to *restore* the states to the Union rather than
how to govern them.[61]

By 1867 moderates were convinced that Negro suffrage was
necessary to secure freedmen's civil rights, and this conviction
provided a basis for the Military Reconstruction Act of March
1867. The act grew out of three separate proposals: a radical
bill to reorganize the states and effect an internal political revolution; a moderate plan to readmit the states when they ratified
the Fourteenth Amendment; and a new proposal to create military government in the South for the purpose of maintaining law
and order and protecting blacks and Unionists. Although this
third measure was not initially sponsored by the radicals, they
quickly adopted it as their own, and the compromise that finally
produced the Reconstruction Act of 1867 combined the moderate promise to readmit former rebel states upon approval of the
Fourteenth Amendment, the new plan for temporary military

61. Ibid., 214.

control, and the radical demand for new state constitutions based on and guaranteeing Negro suffrage. In effect the moderate Republicans' commitment to the local autonomy of federalism led them to change their opinion on the wisdom and expediency of extending political rights to the freedmen. Previously opposed to universal Negro suffrage, they now saw it as the only way to guarantee freedmen's civil rights without permanent federal intervention in local affairs.

Although the Reconstruction Act imposed demands on the states, it allowed them latitude in responding to the proffered terms. The moderates persisted in thinking that the formation of state governments must be the result of the voluntary action of the people.[62] Accordingly they preferred not to define the steps to be followed in organizing new state governments. Radicals were eager to control the process as closely as possible, but were unable to do so. Although the Reconstruction Act declared the existing southern governments provisional only and subject to the paramount authority of the United States, in effect it recognized the validity of those governments by ignoring the question of procedures for calling constitutional conventions and reforming state governments. Adhering to the idea of voluntarism, Congress allowed the states to respond to the act according to their own devices. Indeed, voluntarism was more apparent in this measure than in the Wade-Davis bill of 1864, which carefully specified reorganization steps and machinery. Only when President Johnson vetoed the Reconstruction Act did Congress pass another measure taking control of reorganization away from the state governments and giving it to the army. Even then, however, Congress gave southerners options on calling conventions and approving new state constitutions.[63]

In 1868 accumulated hostility against the President and fear that he would undermine the reconstruction process led to Johnson's impeachment trial. After his acquittal, Republicans at once saw the wisdom of readmitting the seceded states, lest the

62. Ibid., 229.
63. Perman, *Reunion Without Compromise*, 272.

President use his military power under the Reconstruction acts to promote conservative ends. Congress therefore passed enabling acts restoring the states to the Union upon acceptance of the fundamental condition that they should never amend their constitutions to disfranchise Negroes. In this way Congress for the first time attempted to control the states *after* their restoration to the Union, but even as these enabling acts were being formulated lawmakers recognized that they were unenforceable.[64] By the end of 1868, with all but three states restored, the focus of reconstruction politics shifted to the states. National reconstruction policy was essentially complete.

Throughout the period 1861 to 1868 Republicans asserted federal supremacy but were keenly sensitive to the imperatives of state-centered federalism. Intent upon repudiating the theory of state sovereignty and establishing federal power as concurrent with and then ultimately superior to that of the states in the sphere of civil rights, they nevertheless acknowledged states' rights. It was not their purpose to consolidate legislative power and create a unitary government.

Constitutional theory expressed the moderate position that most congressmen adopted on questions of federalism. The grasp of war theory, for example, argued that the federal government held the states temporarily under the war power, and could demand changes within the states in order to secure the results of the war. This approach gave the federal government great power, but it also recognized the existence of the states and the principle of local autonomy. Proponents of the theory expected southerners voluntarily to agree to changes through state constitutional and legislative action, thereby guaranteeing a secure reunion. In a widely publicized statement of the grasp of war theory, the noted legal writer and publicist Richard H. Dana in 1865 said the people of the South were in possession of their original constituent powers and must meet in conventions to form new constitutions. Denying any intention of exercising sovereign civil jurisdiction over the states, Dana anticipated the

64. Benedict, *A Compromise of Principle*, 319–20.

resumption of traditional state powers subject only to the limitations of the federal constitution.[65]

During the war and Reconstruction the guarantee clause of the Constitution provided an alternative basis for federal power over state reorganization. Because the guarantee clause could be interpreted as a source of permanent federal power to intervene in state affairs, it appealed after the war to radical Republicans who earlier had argued for territorialization and state suicide.[66] Most congressmen did not view the clause in this way, however, but rather regarded it as a source of temporary federal power for supervising the formation of state governments. The language of the clause, as noted earlier, created a presumption that the states were still in the Union, and most lawmakers believed that under the authority it provided Congress could, through enabling acts, permit states whose governments had been overthrown to reestablish civil authority in accordance with the Constitution.

Both of these theories of federal power entered into the debate over reconstruction. Dana, for example, explaining that the nation held the seceded states in the grasp of war, said the object of Congressional legislation was to form republican governments acceptable to the nation.[67] Important as the grasp of war theory was, however, the guarantee clause was the favored basis for state reorganization. Thus the report of the Joint Committee on Reconstruction in 1866, though it blurred the theoretical issue of the status of the states in order to satisfy various factions within the Republican party, adhered to the guarantee clause conception of reconstruction. Declaring that the states were deprived of legitimate civil governments, the Joint Committee held that the people must form and ratify new constitutions that would establish republican government. The committee stated further that while the federal government

65. Richard H. Dana, Jr., *Speech at Faneuil Hall, June 21, 1865* (Boston, 1865), 1–4; Benedict, "Preserving the Constitution: The Conservative Basis of Radical Reconstruction," loc. cit., 69–74.

66. Ibid., 74.

67. Wiecek, *The Guarantee Clause of the U.S. Constitution*, 190–91.

would determine the fundamental conditions, the people in the states should voluntarily accept the elements of a new republican order. The guarantee clause, in short, offered a middle ground between exclusive federal control of reconstruction and complete local autonomy or self-reconstruction, such as had resulted from President Johnson's policy of 1865. The report of the Joint Committee in June 1866 represented the high point of development of the guarantee clause, while the Reconstruction Act of 1867 marked the culmination of appeals to the clause as a sound and moderate basis for state reorganization.[68]

The persistence of voluntarism and state-centered federalism in Congressional thinking was evidence of the kind of constitutional conservatism that kept reconstruction policy from veering off into revolutionary radicalism. Not only were radicals unable to territorialize the South, they also failed to confiscate rebel property, distribute land to the freedmen, or disfranchise former Confederates in any comprehensive way. The very nature of the legislative process forced compromises between the radicals and other factions within the Republican party. As a result, the major pieces of postwar legislation, including the Reconstruction Act of 1867, usually regarded as the epitome of radicalism, were moderate measures.[69] On the other hand, the fact that voluntarism and state action were parts of a policy that from the radical point of view produced uncertain not to say unsatisfactory results by allowing southerners room to maneuver and opportunities to be recalcitrant, has led some historians to argue that it was too conservative. According to this view, outright subjugation of the South would have been more effective than the irresolute policy that Congress attempted. By denying white southerners any choice at all in the matter, Congress could have reconstructed the states in such a way as to protect Negro civil rights.[70]

For all its constitutional conservatism, however, and despite

68. Ibid., 200–06.
69. Benedict, "Preserving the Constitution: The Conservative Basis of Radical Reconstruction," loc. cit., 82–84, n. 38.
70. Cf. Perman, *Reunion Without Compromise.*

the fact that many radical demands went unfulfilled, Congressional reconstruction contained elements that when viewed in historical perspective were undeniably radical. Repudiation of state sovereignty, the limitation of state powers over personal liberty and civil rights, and the extension of civil and political equality to Negroes may seem less radical than the confiscation and land allotment plans that Congress rejected after the war. But they were exceedingly radical when measured against the antebellum conditions of blacks that most people considered the relevant basis for comparison in evaluating the postwar situation. Furthermore, there is no good reason to believe that a policy of subjugation would have caused white southerners to change their minds and accept blacks as equal citizens, or that it would have precluded a reaction such as occurred in the 1870s and after.[71]

If for the sake of argument one accepts the view that reconstruction failed, it is more reasonable to place responsibility for the failure on President Johnson for not encouraging white southerners to accept the Republican terms of 1866–67, or on southerners themselves for rejecting the terms, rather than on Republican lawmakers who gave the latter a choice in the matter. The federalist tradition of local self-government, combined with the belief that successful reconstruction must include an element of reconciliation, gave constitutional and political plausibility to postwar Congressional policy. If the Union of republican states was to be restored, as everyone assumed, and if a rational relationship existed between ends and means, then it was of the utmost importance to include in the plan of reunification a component of voluntarism and local participation. To ignore this consideration, as proponents of subjugation were prepared to do, was to run the risk of abandoning the very purpose for which the war had been fought—the preservation of republican Unionism—by employing unrepublican means in guaranteeing its results.

71. LaWanda Cox, "Reconstruction Foredoomed? The Policy of Southern Consent," *Reviews in American History*, I (December, 1973), 541–47.

5

The Nationalization of Civil Rights, 1865-1883

~~~~~~

DURING RECONSTRUCTION the issue of civil rights, like the question of emancipation in wartime politics, was both a means of securing fundamental political objectives and an ideological end in itself. Protecting freedmen's rights was first of all a necessary means of confirming the abolition of slavery and extending democratic institutions into the South. Black civil rights also possessed instrumental value in a more expedient political sense related to the fact that voting came to be seen as a right of citizenship rather than, as previously, a privilege granted to certain citizens on a prudential basis by the responsible political community. The expediency inherent in this change lay in the certainty that newly enfranchised freedmen would support the party that gave them the right to vote. At the same time, however, freedmen's rights became an ideological and moral issue, a matter of justice as well as expediency. Indeed many Republican congressmen defended Negro civil rights not for political gain but rather in spite of the political risk it involved. A more favorable view of blacks as a result of emancipation notwithstanding, racial prejudice remained deeply embedded in social practices.

Although decisions taken during Reconstruction laid the foundation for modern American civil rights law, the term civil rights carried a different meaning in the 1860's than it does in the twentieth century. Nowadays civil rights and civil liberties have been conflated and are essentially interchangeable terms. Civil liberties refers to legal guarantees which protect individuals against governmental interference in a variety of freedoms that are mainly political in nature, such as freedom of speech, press, petition, and assembly. Civil rights refers to legal rules that protect individuals in their ordinary social and economic pursuits against injury or impediment from other private individuals as well as from government. But civil rights have also acquired a political connotation, so that interference with a person's attempt to exercise free speech or to vote is a violation of civil rights as well as civil liberties.

In the nineteenth century the ideas of civil liberty and civil rights were not political as they are now. Civil liberty was the general condition of a free individual in civil society, and it consisted in the right of all citizens, equally and without hindrance from government, to move about, work and enjoy the rewards of labor, own or rent property, make contracts and participate in the market place, bring suit and testify in courts of law, maintain whatever religious beliefs and practices one wished, and enjoy the benefits of marriage and the family. These specific rights, largely economic in character, were ordinary civil rights, and they were defined and regulated by state, county, and local law and custom. Political rights, though no less subject to state and local regulation, stood in contrast to civil rights. The rights to vote, hold office, and serve on juries were in a legal sense not so much rights as privileges conferred on certain individuals by the political community on the basis of expediency and the public good. In further contrast to civil rights stood social rights, which referred to the sphere of personal relationships and associations, either private or public, in which personal taste or prejudice held sway and into which the law did not enter. It is thus obvious that civil rights meant substantially less in the 1860s than they do today. Although the sharp distinction between civil and political rights began to disappear during Reconstruction as Congress, often in the same measures, tried to protect the right to vote and the right to make contracts, civil rights were still basically economic rather than political in nature.

Within this theoretical framework, Congress in 1866–67,

under the direction of Republican party moderates, created legal guarantees of black people's civil rights. Through national legislation, enlargement of national court jurisdiction, and amendment of the national constitution, it defined the status of Negroes as citizens of the United States whose rights the Union government could legitimately, if in limited ways, protect. No longer the exclusive concern of the states, civil rights became nationalized. Yet this nationalization of civil rights, like the process of reorganizing state governments in the South, carefully respected the traditional federal character of the constitutional order. Concerned to safeguard freedmen's rights, national policy makers also recognized the value of local autonomy and self-government in the American political culture. Accordingly, evincing a constitutional outlook that can best be described as state-rights nationalism, Congress established as a principal meaning of national citizenship the right of equality before the law in the diverse state jurisdictions that federalism encouraged.

Long before the fighting ended, the rights of emancipated slaves became inextricably tied to Reconstruction policy. The Wade-Davis bill of 1864, proposing to guarantee personal liberty and equal rights in reorganized southern states, spoke directly to the issue, and the Freedmen's Bureau Act of 1865, giving the ex-slaves temporary legal protection and welfare assistance, implicitly recognized their status as citizens. Still, these measures were concerned mainly with wartime exigencies. A more direct attempt to settle the question of freedmen's rights came in the framing and adoption of the Thirteenth Amendment.

Introduced in 1864 as the constitutionally necessary capstone of military emancipation, the Thirteenth Amendment declared that neither slavery nor involuntary servitude, except as a punishment for crime, shall exist within the United States or its territories. The amendment further gave Congress power to enforce this prohibition by appropriate legislation. Approved by the necessary two-thirds vote of the Senate in April 1864, the amendment finally passed the House of Representatives on January 31, 1865. Three-fourths of the states, including seven former Confederate states, ratified the amendment by December 1865.

Transparent as the meaning of the Thirteenth Amendment seems today, it gave rise to troublesome questions of interpretation at the time it was adopted. If it was obvious that the prohibition of slavery placed vast numbers of blacks in a new condition of freedom, it was by no means clear precisely what other civil rights it conferred upon them. Similar uncertainty arose concerning the nature and extent of Congressional power to enforce the amendment, an understandable perplexity since this was the first formal constitutional expansion of federal power since the beginning of the government. The answers to these questions of course depended on how slavery was defined. During the war, when the amendment was framed, this had seemed self-evident, but it ceased to be so self-evident after the war when the southern states under President Johnson's reconstruction policy began to legislate a new civil status for the emancipated slaves.

Adopting a narrow view of slavery as chattelism, Republican lawmakers in framing the Thirteenth Amendment intended to make it impossible for persons to be held as property. Conceived of in this way, the amendment conferred a right of personal liberty; that is, the right to own one's person and to exercise the elementary power of locomotion. It was impossible, however, to confine Thirteenth Amendment liberty within such narrow limits. A moment's thought suggested that bare personal liberty needed to be buttressed about with other rights in order to fulfill the promise of emancipation. Accordingly Republican congressmen argued that the amendment would confer fundamental civil rights on the freed slaves: the right to labor and enjoy the fruits of their labor, to own property, to bring suit and testify in courts of law, to enter into marriage and receive the protection of the private household, to speak and write freely and to become educated. The amendment would, in short, extend to the ex-slaves all the nonpolitical rights implied in the phrase "life, liberty, and the pursuit of happiness." The emancipated slave, summarized the New York *Tribune*, would take his place as a citizen of the republic "endowed with the same feelings and rights, and subject to the same duties as other citizens."[1]

Congressmen found it easier to describe the new condition of freedom than to say how its many aspects would be realized. To argue that the Thirteenth Amendment conferred ordinary civil rights required a broader definition of slavery as the denial of fundamental natural rights rather than merely as chattelism. It followed that the power which the amendment conferred to prohibit slavery was in reality a grant of power to protect civil rights by positive legislation. By 1866 this conclusion seemed irresistible, but it is important to note that in framing and adopting the amendment in 1864–65 few Republicans made such a broad claim for federal power. They said Congress could legislate to protect personal liberty—the right not to be held as property—but beyond this minimal claim most of them were unwilling or unable to go. Nor was this decision thoughtless or unconsidered. When Senator Charles Sumner of Massachusetts proposed a far more radical antislavery amendment stating that all people were equal before the law and giving Congress power to enforce this legal equality by appropriate legislation, Republican leaders opposed it. In their view the point was simply to take away from the states the power to recognize and protect chattel slavery, and give the federal government a new and concurrent power to guarantee personal liberty.

The history of the Northwest Ordinance, from which the prohibitory language of the Thirteenth Amendment was drawn, supported a narrow view of the scope and effect of federal power under the amendment. Throughout the antebellum period the Ordinance was interpreted only as a source of personal liberty, not of civil rights in any broader sense. The arguments of conservative opponents of the Thirteenth Amendment suggest that the original intention of its framers was similarly narrow. Democrats professed fear that the amendment would irrevocably alter the federal-state balance, but what they ob-

1. New York *Tribune*, February 6, 1865.

jected to was the use of the amending power to give the federal government concurrent authority over personal liberty. They did not, in other words, fear that the grant of power to enforce the prohibition of slavery would be interpreted broadly as a plenary power to legislate on the range of civil rights that surrounded strict personal liberty. Republicans as well as Democrats seemed to assume that these rights, in the penumbra of personal liberty, would remain within the jurisdiction of the states.

So rapidly did events after Appomattox overtake the perceptions and expectations on which the framing of the Thirteenth Amendment rested that it might be thought of as the unknown or forgotten amendment. In retrospect the amendment marks the starting point of modern civil rights law and policy; along with the Fourteenth and Fifteenth Amendments it provided the legal foundations for notable changes in the status of blacks in the twentieth century. To contemporaries, however, the amendment signified culmination rather than commencement. It marked the end of the antislavery movement and appeared as the great reform that would purify the republic. Not only would it give liberty to a whole race, it would also enlarge and improve the liberty of white Americans by removing the obstacles to free speech, a free press, and free travel that the defense of slavery had thrown up in the South. Most people saw the Thirteenth Amendment moreover as the necessary and sufficient basis for reconstruction. Once the southern states accepted this momentous constitutional change, wrote publicist Henry Everett Russell in September 1864, disagreement about the proper method of restoring the states to the Union would end.[2]

As the former rebel states regained local control under President Johnson's reconstruction policy, however, they fixed the status and rights of the freed people in ways far different from what Republicans had hoped for or anticipated. While the Black Codes which the states enacted in late 1865 and early

2. Henry Everett Russell, "The Constitutional Amendment," *Continental Monthly*, VI (September 1864), 315–26.

1866 gave blacks rights that had hitherto been denied them, the relevant political truth was that the codes represented an attempt to make the freedmen in effect slaves of the community by treating them as a distinct class and by severely restricting their access to the ordinary civil rights and liberties that white persons enjoyed. When Congress met in December 1865, it was apparent that policies which white southerners thought showed a willingness to accept emancipation threatened in Republican eyes to make a mockery of Thirteenth Amendment liberty, if not actually to restore slavery. These circumstances forced Republicans, as they perceived the need for federal power to protect the freedmen against injury and discrimination, to reconsider the implications of the Thirteenth Amendment.

In the alarming situation that faced the black people of the South in early 1866, Congress first tried to protect civil rights by strengthening the Freedmen's Bureau. Organized in May 1865 to provide emergency welfare relief for the former slaves, the Bureau by the end of the year was exercising judicial power in local affairs on behalf of the freed blacks. In order to confirm this protective function, which was not authorized by the act of Congress creating the Bureau in March 1865, Republicans in February 1866 passed the second Freedmen's Bureau Act.[3] The Freedmen's Bureau, however, an agency in the War Department, derived its authority from the war power and legally could do no more than provide temporary protection and support. The necessity of providing permanent civil guarantees of freedmen's rights remained.

The quest for a nonmilitary solution to the problem of freedmen's rights resulted in the Civil Rights Act of 1866. As they watched the progress of southern reconstruction, Republicans arrived at new insights into the nature and scope of federal power under the Thirteenth Amendment. Alarmed at the restrictions that the Black Codes imposed on the former slaves, most of them now reached the conclusion that Congress could

3. Johnson vetoed the bill and Congress passed it over his veto in July 1866.

legislate to secure not only strict personal liberty, but also nec-essarily related civil rights. In effect this meant adopting a broader view of slavery as the denial of fundamental civil rights. Thus the Republican journalist William M. Grosvenor argued in October 1865 that the Thirteenth Amendment promised no mere nominal freedom but full protection in the rights of person and property and absolute equality before the law. Congress-man James A. Garfield of Ohio, in a typical expression of the new view of the constitutional amendment that prevailed in 1866, declared that so far from being the bare privilege of not being chained, freedom comprehended a wide array of rights which Congress could guarantee by positive legislation.[4]

The starting point for protecting freedmen's rights was insis-tence that the former slaves were citizens of the United States. For many years of course the question of Negro citizenship had been a vexing issue. Some states regarded blacks as citizens entitled to basic legal protection in their person and property; other states, while recognizing that blacks had certain minimal rights, denied that they were citizens.[5] In the Dred Scott case the Supreme Court resolved the question by declaring that Ne-groes were not citizens of the United States, though they were not aliens either. During the Civil War congressional military legislation regarded blacks as part of the people of the United States, or as citizens, and Attorney General Edward Bates is-sued an opinion stating that free Negroes were United States

4. William M. Grosvenor, "The Rights of the Nation, and the Duty of Congress," *New Englander*, XXIV (October 1865), 769; B. A. Hins-dale, ed., *The Works of James Abram Garfield* (2 vols.; Boston, 1882), I, 86.

5. The trouble was that no clear definition of citizenship could be agreed on. Northerners tended to view it as a condition of equality, en-joyed by all who were born in the United States, which entitled a person to protection of basic civil rights. Southerners defined it more narrowly as a condition which entitled a person to all the rights and privileges conferred on the highest class in society, thus including political privi-leges. This seemingly technical question of state citizenship was im-portant because if a person were determined to be a citizen of a state, he could be regarded as a citizen of the United States and entitled to national protection under the privileges and immunities clause of the federal Constitution (Art. IV, Sec. 2).

citizens. These measures were not legally conclusive, however, so that when the former Confederate states began in 1865 to define the rights of the freedmen, an authoritative decision establishing Negro citizenship under the Constitution became imperative. Accordingly the Civil Rights Act of 1866, in its opening section, declared that all persons born or naturalized in the United States, except Indians not taxed, were citizens of the United States.

The particular rights of citizenship which needed federal protection were not in dispute among Republicans. Since early in the war discussions of emancipation had produced a firm distinction between civil rights on the one hand and political and social rights on the other. Disavowing any intention of conferring the latter, Republicans confined their attention to the protection of person and property. Thus the Civil Rights Act declared that citizens of the United States, irrespective of race, color, or previous condition of servitude, should have the same right in every state to make and enforce contracts, sue, be parties and give evidence, and inherit, purchase, lease, or sell property. In draft form the act contained a further general prohibition of discrimination by states "in civil rights and immunities" on account of race or color. Democrats and several Republicans objected to this comprehensive guarantee, however, on the ground that it would prevent states from making any legal distinction at all between Negroes and whites. It might even confer political equality on the freedmen. With moderates in control, Republicans met these objections by removing the general civil rights guarantee. In its final form therefore the act enumerated specific civil rights and, at its most general, promised "full and equal benefit of all laws and proceedings for the security of person and property," the same as was enjoyed by white citizens.

It was not the meaning of civil rights, but rather the nature and scope of federal power to protect the rights of citizens under the Thirteenth Amendment that was uncertain in 1866. Some radical Republicans argued that if Negroes were citizens and possessed rights under the federal Constitution, then it stood to reason that the federal government could protect those rights by positive legislation against infringement from any source. In support of this position radicals cited the famous antebellum case of Prigg v. Pennsylvania and the doctrine that Congress could punish any interference with constitutionally secured rights. Carried to its logical conclusion the argument contends that the Thirteenth Amendment nationalized personal liberty and civil rights by giving Congress plenary legislative power to protect civil rights against violations by either state governments or private citizens.[6] In fact, however, nationalization of civil rights through the Thirteenth Amendment was not so sweeping as this view suggests, because most Republicans, as well as being concerned to protect Negro rights, were opposed to federal assumption of local criminal jurisdiction to the extent that legislation against private discrimination would have required. They interpreted the antislavery amendment as giving Congress power to legislate only against state action that denied Negroes civil rights.

This state action qualification on federal power appeared in a provision of the Civil Rights Act which stated that any person who under color of law, statute, ordinance, regulation, or custom deprived any inhabitant of rights secured by the act was guilty of a misdemeanor and on conviction was subject to fine and imprisonment. Although private injury and discrimination against blacks were serious problems, most congressmen believed the state governments were the chief source of difficulty. The states were primarily responsible for protecting civil liberty, and their officers influenced the behavior of local communities. If the states could be made to respect Negro rights, private wrongs would be taken care of through the enforcement of municipal laws for the protection of person and property. Re-

6. See, for example, Jacobus ten Broek, *Equal Under Law* (New York, 1965); Howard Jay Graham, *Everyman's Constitution: Historical Essays on the Fourteenth Amendment, the "Conspiracy Theory," and American Constitutionalism* (Madison, Wis., 1968); Robert J. Kaczorowski, "The Nationlization of Civil Rights: Constitutional Theory and Practice in a Racist Society, 1866–1883," Ph.D. dissertation, University of Minnesota, 1971.

publicans naively believed that private violations would cease when it became clear that they would be punished. Senator Lyman Trumbull of Illinois, principal drafter of the Civil Rights Act, offered this analysis when he said that it would be necessary only to "subject to fine and imprisonment one or two in a state, and the most prominent ones I should hope at that, to break up this whole business."[7] In similar vein Representative James Wilson of Iowa, when asked why the civil rights bill directed its sanctions only against state officers and not the entire community, said it was because Congress was not legislating a general criminal code for the states.[8]

Republican opposition to direct federal regulation of civil rights was evident also in the repeated observation that the Civil Rights Act would cease to have effect when the states assumed the protective function they were supposed to under the Constitution. The potential onus of the act was considerable. Not only could state officers end up in jail, but cases involving persons who were unable to enforce in state courts rights secured by the act could also be removed to federal courts. National courts also had exclusive jurisdiction of offenses against the act. These varied impacts could be avoided, however, if the states passed laws securing legal equality for blacks, and if they made no discrimination in enforcing local laws for the protection of person and property.[9] Like the Freedmen's Bureau Act, the Civil Rights Act in other words was intended as a temporary measure which Republicans hoped would induce the states to recognize Negroes as citizens. Observing that Congress could pass laws securing freedmen's rights and have them enforced through the army and the courts, the Springfield *Weekly Republican* predicted that the South would learn that if it wanted to be rid of federal interference "it must, in good faith, protect its own citizens. . . ."[10]

7. *Cong. Globe*, 39 Cong., 1 Sess., 475 (January 29, 1866).
8. Ibid., 1118–1120 (March 1, 1866).
9. Ibid., 600 (February 2, 1866), remarks of Lyman Trumbull, 1833–37 (April 7, 1866), remarks of William Stewart.
10. Springfield *Weekly Republican*, December 23, 1865, editorial.

Through national legislation Congress thus intended to make Negroes equal before state law as United States citizens. Blacks would stand upon an equality in national law, but the important practical meaning of this equality was to secure equal rights within states, or intrastate equality. Because no one questioned federalism as the basic structure of the constitutional system, no one thought of Congress as the legislature of a unitary nation. Nationalization of civil rights did not mean centralized law-making and administration, but rather state recognition and enforcement of equal rights under a general guarantee from the federal government, as in the Civil Rights Act. It was no part of Republican thinking, observed the New York *Post* in 1866, to legislate a criminal code for the states, or to establish rules for giving evidence or holding property or protecting citizens in their occupations.[11] But whatever laws states passed regulating or guaranteeing ordinary liberties must be applied impartially and for the benefit of both races equally.[12] To put the matter another way, every American citizen had a right under the federal Constitution to make contracts, for example, but the specific rules for entering into a particular contract were left to state determination and would vary from state to state. In the words of Lyman Trumbull, the states might grant or withhold such specific civil rights as they pleased, provided they did so irrespective of race and did not abridge fundamental rights under the Constitution. The Civil Rights Act would not interfere with the municipal regulations of any state that protected all alike in the rights of person and property, Trumbull asserted.[13]

The doctrine of a qualified and concurrent federal power over civil rights complemented and in part derived from the Republican conception of dual citizenship. Of the existence of state citizenship going back to the formation of the Union in 1776 there could be no doubt. Because state sovereignty advo-

11. New York *Evening Post*, cited in Baltimore *American*, March 30, 1866.
12. Ibid.
13. *Cong. Globe*, 39 Cong., 1 Sess., 1760 (April 4, 1866).

cates insisted that only the states could command allegiance, however, there was less certainty concerning federal citizenship, despite express reference in the Constitution to citizens of the United States. Furthermore, when the reality of national citizenship was recognized, orthodox legal doctrine considered it derivative of citizenship in the states. In the Civil Rights Act, therefore, and again in the Fourteenth Amendment, Congress established the existence of national citizenship beyond any question and made state citizenship derivative of it. But rather than two clearly separate citizenships, lawmakers thought of a single entity—American citizenship—which assumed two complementary aspects, national and state.

In its national aspect American citizenship was a title to fundamental civil rights under the Constitution, such as the right to own property, which the Civil Rights Act identified. From this national right flowed the right as a state citizen to enjoy equality in respect of a state's criminal and civil code. Thinking in these terms, the Philadelphia *North American* refuted the idea that state and federal citizenship were separate legal entities; on the contrary, they were essentially the same.[14] According to Republican arguments in 1866, the federal government through the Thirteenth Amendment assumed power and responsibility for protecting the civil rights surrounding personal liberty. This power was not primary, original, or direct, however, as in a unitary government, but rather corrective, supervisory, and indirect. It was intended to guarantee state performance in providing equality before the law with respect to ordinary civil rights. When states denied citizens' rights by enactments such as the Black Codes, or when they denied equal protection by failing to uphold rights or administer justice impartially, as occurred so egregiously in the 1870s, the federal government could intervene to secure civil rights. In substance and practical effect therefore, national citizenship consisted in equality before the law as a state citizen.

The excited political situation in 1866 gave urgency to the

14. Philadelphia *North American*, April 11, 1866.

task of protecting freedmen's rights and plausibility to the new view of federal power under the Thirteenth Amendment on which the Civil Rights Act rested. Accordingly almost all Republicans voted for the measure in April 1866. Nevertheless, a few in the majority party could not agree that the amendment gave Congress even the qualified power over civil rights of which the new law purported to be an exercise. This handful of Republicans insisted, as in 1865, that the power to prohibit slavery, peonage, or any interference with strict personal liberty was one thing, while the power to regulate the domestic relations of life, liberty, and property within the states was something very different.[15] Arguing that the Thirteenth Amendment conferred only the former power, they held that further amendment of the Constitution was necessary to enable Congress to protect ordinary civil rights.

Representative John A. Bingham of Ohio, the chief spokesman for this minority Republican point of view, offered a constitutional amendment authorizing national civil rights legislation. In its original form Bingham's proposal gave Congress power to "make all laws necessary and proper to secure to the citizens of each State all privileges and immunities of citizens in the several States, and to all persons in the several States equal protection in the rights of life, liberty, and property."[16] Although it appears not to have been Bingham's intention, this language seemed unequivocally to transfer legislative power over civil rights from the states to the federal government, thus revolutionizing federal-state relations. As a member of the Joint Committee on Reconstruction, Bingham subsequently revised his proposal and employed the state action formula of the Civil Rights Act. In its final form therefore section 1 of the Fourteenth Amendment declared that "No state shall make or en-

15. *Cong. Globe*, 39 Cong., 1 Sess., Appendix, 158 (March 8, 1866), remarks of Columbus Delano.

16. Ibid., 1034 (February 26, 1866). Bingham introduced his proposal as part of a comprehensive constitutional amendment which the Joint Committee on Reconstruction prepared dealing with representation and the exclusion of former rebels. Eventually of course this became the Fourteenth Amendment.

force any law which shall abridge the privileges or immunities of citizens of the United States; nor shall any State deprive any person of life, liberty, or property without due process of law; nor deny to any person within its jurisdiction the equal protection of the laws." Section 5 of the amendment gave Congress power to enforce this tripartite requirement by appropriate legislation.

According to Thaddeus Stevens, the amendment meant that if a state distinguished between different classes of citizens in its laws, Congress could correct the discrimination and inequality.[17] Without denying states primary jurisdiction over civil rights, it gave the federal government power to guarantee equality in the way states regulated the rights of American citizenship. As for the content of the rights referred to in section 1 of the amendment, most Republicans viewed the trilogy of privileges and immunities, due process, and equal protection of the laws as a caption for the rights enumerated in the Civil Rights Act.[18]

Congress approved the Fourteenth Amendment and sent it to the states for ratification in June 1866. Meanwhile federal officials used the Civil Rights Act and the second Freedmen's-Bureau Act, passed over President Johnson's veto in July 1866, to confirm and strengthen administrative expedients devised earlier to protect the freedmen against the Black Codes and other forms of discrimination and injury. These enforcement efforts constituted the initial application and interpretation of federal power under the Civil Rights Act, and they were followed by federal court rulings which further elaborated the nature and scope of federal civil rights authority under the Thirteenth Amendment.

Postwar federal protection of freedmen's rights began in May 1865 when General O. O. Howard, head of the Freed-

17. Ibid., 1063 (February 27, 1866).
18. Herman Belz, *A New Birth of Freedom: The Republican Party and Freedmen's Rights, 1861 to 1866* (Westport, Conn., 1976), 172–74; Alexander M. Bickel, "The Original Understanding and the Segregation Decision," *Harvard Law Review*, LXIX (November 1955), 56–65; Charles Fairman, *Reconstruction and Reunion, 1864–88, Part One* (New York, 1971), 1281–90.

men's Bureau, ordered Bureau agents to remove from state courts and assume jurisdiction of disputes involving emancipated slaves. Freedmen's Bureau courts thus came into existence under the military authority of the War Department, but the Department withdrew these courts as states resumed control of local affairs throughout 1865.[19] President Johnson challenged protection of freedmen in Freedmen's Bureau courts and military tribunals in April 1866 when he issued a proclamation announcing the official end of the rebellion and stating that the Civil courts should handle disputes involving civilians. Unwilling to acquiesce in Johnson's policy, Secretary of War Edwin M. Stanton and General Ulysses S. Grant instructed military commanders to use their authority under the Freedmen's Bureau, Civil Rights, and Habeas Corpus Acts to provide military tribunals for freedmen and Unionists who were denied justice in state courts. In July 1866 Grant ordered commanders to arrest and hold for trial in federal courts persons charged with crimes against blacks whom state authorities failed to apprehend.[20]

The Freedmen's Bureau, the army, and the lower federal courts enforced and interpreted the Civil Rights Act in 1866 and 1867. Military officers arrested and prosecuted persons accused of civil rights violations when state authorities neglected to act, and transferred cases from state to federal courts when prejudice against Negroes made it impossible for them to receive justice in the former. Furthermore under the Reconstruction Act of 1867 military commanders sometimes removed state officers guilty of discrimination against blacks. The impact of these numerous actions in support of civil rights was considerable, though it hardly produced the alteration in race relations that friends of the freedmen hoped for. Discrimination against Negroes still existed among local police authorities and in the

19. George R. Bentley, *A History of the Freedmen's Bureau* (Philadelphia, 1955), 156.

20. Harold M. Hyman, "Johnson, Stanton, and Grant: A Reconsideration of the Army's Role in the Events Leading to Impeachment," *American Historical Review*, LXVI (October 1960), 85–100; Kaczorowski, "The Nationalization of Civil Rights," 127.

civil courts, and many state and local officials entirely disregarded the Civil Rights Act. Considering the widespread prejudice against blacks throughout the society, however, the attempt to guarantee their civil rights was impressive. Certainly the undertaking was novel and unprecedented, and it signified important changes in southern society. Freedmen's Bureau agents adjudicated thousands of cases involving blacks and acted on hundreds of thousands of complaints. In enforcing the Civil Rights Act moreover the Bureau induced the states to change their laws to provide at least formal legal equality for blacks with respect to testifying and bringing suit in state courts.[21]

In applying the Civil Rights Act, military and Freedmen's Bureau authorities interpreted it substantially as Republican lawmakers intended with respect to the state action limitation on congressional power. As the act provided, federal authorities arrested state officers and judges who discriminated against blacks, and when state courts discriminated in cases involving Negroes, federal tribunals assumed jurisdiction of the cases on removal.[22] In some instances federal officials arrested private individuals, but here too the constitutional justification of federal intervention was state action, to wit, the state's denial of freedmen's rights through its failure to apprehend persons who committed crimes against Negroes. Federal power did not, in other words, supersede state power in any categorical way, but rather operated to correct state denial of rights when it took the form of neglect or omission as well as when it assumed the form of positive legislation. Although Republicans did not regard negative state action as the major problem, they had anticipated it in framing the Civil Rights Act.[23]

Judicial application and interpretation of the Civil Rights Act also agreed with the congressional view of federal power under the Thirteenth Amendment. In an important circuit court

21. Bentley, *A History of the Freedmen's Bureau*, 156–58.
22. Kaczorowski, "The Nationalization of Civil Rights," 131.
23. *Cong. Globe*, 39 Cong., 1 Sess., 1833 (April 7, 1866), remarks of William Lawrence.

decision in Maryland in 1867, Chief Justice Salmon P. Chase declared that a black child was illegally held as an apprentice under state authority in violation of the Civil Rights Act and the Thirteenth Amendment. Apprenticeships for blacks, Chase observed, violated the new civil rights law by failing to provide the same security and benefits that were available under state law to white apprentices. Approving the law as a proper exercise of congressional power under the Thirteenth Amendment, Chase held further that the Maryland apprenticeship system amounted to involuntary servitude within the meaning of the amendment.[24]

In the well known case of U.S. v. Rhodes the federal circuit court for Kentucky also found the Civil Rights Act constitutional under the Thirteenth Amendment. The federal court received this case, involving the trial of several white persons for burglary against a Negro, on removal from a state court because Kentucky law, in violation of the Civil Rights Act, did not permit blacks to testify. In a sweeping decision Supreme Court Justice Noah Swayne interpreted the Thirteenth Amendment not only as a prohibition of chattelism but also, in accordance with the new view of the amendment that prevailed in 1866, as a guarantee of "free institutions." Swayne judged it appropriate therefore for Congress to enact the Civil Rights Act to prevent legislative oppression of blacks, as in the Kentucky statute.[25]

From 1867 to 1870 the civil rights question became absorbed in the larger and more explosive issues of Negro suffrage

24. In Re Turner, 24 *Federal Cases* 337 (1867); Richard L. Curry, ed., *Radicalism, Racism, and Party Realignment: The Border States during Reconstruction* (Baltimore, 1969), 154–56.

25. U.S. *v.* Rhodes, 27 *Federal Cases* 785 (1866); Victor B. Howard, "The Black Testimony Controversy in Kentucky, 1866–1872," *Journal of Negro History*, LVIII (April 1973), 152–53. State court interpretation of the Civil Rights Act was mixed. Some courts upheld it as valid under the Thirteenth Amendment, as in Maryland, Georgia, and California, while others found it unconstitutional, as in Kentucky. Harold M. Hyman, *A More Perfect Union: The Impact of the Civil War and Reconstruction on the Constitution* (New York, 1973), 484–86; Robert J. Kaczorowski, "Civil Rights and the Federal Courts during Reconstruction" (unpublished paper), 6–7.

and political control of the former Confederate states. The desire to protect freedmen and white Unionists, in conjunction with the necessity of restoring the states to the Union, in 1867 produced the Military Reconstruction Act. Under this law Congress gave voting rights to Negroes in the former rebel states and affirmed the authority of military and Freedmen's Bureau officials to assume jurisdiction of cases in which Negroes were discriminated against in state courts. In 1869 the same dual concern for freedmen's rights and political security, coupled with constitutional hostility toward maintaining a permanent federal presence in the South in order to guarantee blacks' civil rights, led to the passage of the Fifteenth Amendment. Viewed by Republicans as a measure that would enable blacks themselves to vindicate their legal and civil equality, the amendment conferred the right not to be discriminated against in voting because of race, color, or previous condition of servitude. Furthermore, although in a constitutional sense the amendment allowed control of the suffrage to remain within state jurisdiction, in effect it signified a conflation of civil and political rights. Hereafter voting and other political rights, which had traditionally been seen as privileges granted by the responsible political community, were increasingly regarded as natural rights or rights of citizenship.

As in approving the Thirteenth Amendment, Republicans intended the Fifteenth Amendment to be a conclusive step in Reconstruction. Even more rudely and conspicuously than before, however, events proved this expectation false. Violent white opposition to black civil and political equality appeared with the advent of Negro suffrage in the South and, led by the Ku Klux Klan, reached crisis proportions in 1870–71. In response Congress enacted a series of measures—the enforcement acts—to protect Negro civil and political rights and also to preserve Republican party strength against conservatives who would undo southern reconstruction.

The first of these civil rights enforcement measures, passed in May 1870, implemented the Fifteenth Amendment. As in 1866, Congress's main concern was discriminatory state action.

Directed mainly at state election officials, the act declared that citizens who were otherwise qualified to vote in state and local elections were entitled to do so without distinction of color. The act also reflected, however, the changing nature of the civil rights problem by recognizing private violence. It prohibited and punished private interference with the right to vote, and it contained a section aimed at persons who conspired or went in disguise on public highways to prevent citizens from exercising rights protected by the federal Constitution and laws. Republicans, in other words, directed the act in part at terrorist organizations like the Ku Klux Klan and sought to protect blacks' civil rights against a wider variety of violations than in previous legislation. In February 1871, in the second enforcement act, Congress amended this measure by creating a far-reaching system of national supervision of congressional elections.[26]

These laws failed to arrest the spread of Klan violence. Indeed, the southern situation grew so critical, as terror swept through Alabama, Mississippi, Georgia, and South Carolina, that President Grant in March 1871 asked Congress to take further legislative action. The result was the famous Ku Klux Klan Act of May 1871.

The Ku Klux bill marked an important phase in the constitutional history of civil rights because it saw the Republican party, in trying to contain the private lawlessness of the Klan, go to the very limits of power under the civil rights settlement of 1866. Like the Civil Rights Act of 1866, the Ku Klux bill prohibited the denial of constitutional rights by any person acting under color of any law, statute, ordinance, regulation, custom, or usage of any state. This was of course the customary formula for identifying state action. Section 2 of the bill went further, however, and punished conspiracies of two or more persons to violate constitutional rights by committing murder, robbery, assault and battery, manslaughter, or other crimes. Representative Samuel Shellabarger of Ohio, the author of the

26. *Statutes at Large of the United States,* XVI, 140–46; Hyman, *A More Perfect Union,* 527; *U.S. Statutes at Large,* XVI, 433–40.

bill, defended this application of federal power against individual crimes by arguing that when states failed to punish civil
rights offenders, they denied equal protection of the law in violation of the Fourteenth Amendment. In accordance with this
outlook, section 3 of the bill stated that when domestic violence
obstructed the enforcement of the law and state officials could
not or would not uphold a person's civil rights, the situation
constituted a denial of equal protection of the law. Under those
circumstances the bill authorized the President to suspend the
writ of habeas corpus and use military force to guarantee civil
rights.

In arriving at the civil rights settlement of 1866, Congress
recognized that failure by the state to check private violence
could be a form of state action that denied equal protection in a
constitutional sense. The question now was what federal action
was warranted to correct this kind of passive denial of civil
rights. In contrast to Shellabarger's view, several Republicans
held that Congress could not specify and punish ordinary
crimes, because to do so would supersede the states in their
exercise of the police power. Congress could punish a state
officer who refused to protect civil rights for not discharging his
constitutional duty; it could even punish individuals who
formed a conspiracy against a state officer's attempt to fulfill his
constitutional duty to protect civil rights. But Congress could
not, in the opinion of moderate and conservative Republicans,
assume original jurisdiction over the private rights of persons
and property in the states.[27]

Shellabarger revised the Ku Klux bill to accommodate the
objections of moderate and conservative Republicans. The
amended version contained no reference to specific crimes such
as murder or assault, but instead made denial of equal protection of the law and denial of equal privileges and immunities
crimes punishable by federal authority. The revised bill also

27. Alfred Avins, "The Ku Klux Act of 1871; Some Reflected Light
on State Action and the Fourteenth Amendment," *St. Louis University
Law Journal*, XI (1967), 348.

prohibited the acts of individuals that prevented state officers from giving citizens equal protection of the laws.[28]

In these provisions Congress went to the limits of, but nonetheless remained within, the state action theory of federal power under the Fourteenth Amendment. The amendment nationalized civil rights, but this meant that United States citizens had a general right to equal protection of the law and equal privileges and immunities within states (plus the protection of due process of law, as the Fourteenth Amendment states). Nationalization of civil rights also meant that the federal government could protect these rights against state action in the form of positive legislation or executive conduct, and also in the form of neglect or failure to protect civil rights. Congress could reach private acts that denied civil rights, but such acts became cognizable only insofar as they signified state denial of equal protection. The constitutional wrong was not the act of the private individual (for in this view Congress possessed no original jurisdiction over ordinary crimes) but the failure of the state to prevent crimes against civil rights.[29] Furthermore, although the Ku Klux act dealt with individual actions, the object of Congressional concern was not ordinary private crimes against civil rights. In actuality the Klan and other terrorist organizations were conducting a public campaign against the enforcement of state civil rights laws in relation to blacks and Republican Unionists. So far from being an outbreak of ordinary crimes, Klan actions were a quasi-political movement aimed at removing the Republican party from power.[30]

Initially the federal government enforced the Ku Klux and the other civil rights acts with vigor. President Grant suspended the writ of habeas corpus and sent troops into South Carolina in October 1871, and the newly created Department of Justice

28. Kaczorowski, "The Nationalization of Civil Rights," 183–86; Avins, "The Ku Klux Act of 1871," 355–57.

29. Laurent B. Frantz, "Congressional Power to Enforce the Fourteenth Amendment Against Private Acts," *Yale Law Journal*, LXXIII (July 1964), 1359.

30. Avins, "The Ku Klux Act of 1871," 358, 374.

initiated many prosecutions and won over half its cases from 1870 to 1872.[31] The result was the effective breaking up of the Klan by 1873. Although this accomplishment was significant, it did not end deprivation of Negro rights. White hostility assumed more sophisticated forms, and in the face of continuing prejudice federal civil rights efforts relaxed, in part because Klan terror had been stopped and in part because northern opinion was growing weary of the Reconstruction question. An expression of this changing northern outlook, and an important influence on government policy toward civil rights in the 1870s, was the judicial interpretation of the new civil rights laws and constitutional amendments.

The fundamental constitutional problem that the enforcement acts raised concerned the content of national citizenship and the nature and scope of federal power over the rights of citizens. It was clear that the Thirteenth, Fourteenth, and Fifteenth Amendments gave the federal government new powers to regulate personal liberty and civil and political rights, and that they placed restraints on the states in regard to these matters. What needed to be resolved—what Congress had in effect tried to determine in the enforcement acts of 1870–71—was the precise extent of the alteration in federalism that the amendments produced.

The lower federal courts initially took a broad and approving view of federal civil rights power. In cases in Ohio and Alabama, federal circuit courts upheld section 6 of the enforcement act of May 1870, punishing private denial of civil rights. The rights of free speech and assembly, said Supreme Court Justice William B. Woods, referring to the rights which whites violated by breaking up a black political meeting in Alabama, were privileges and immunities of American citizenship secured by the Fourteenth Amendment. Woods held that under the reconstruction amendments Congress could deal directly with pri-

31. Everette Swinney, "Enforcing the Fifteenth Amendment, 1870–1877," *Journal of Southern History*, XXVIII (May 1962), 202–18.

vate civil rights offenders when states denied equal protection through inaction. In a circuit court decision in Delaware which upheld the first enforcement act against a state election official, Supreme Court Justice William Strong argued that although the Fourteenth and Fifteenth Amendments placed express restrictions on states, in effect they gave Congress power to protect civil rights against interference from any source whatever.[32]

In 1873 federal judges retreated from the theory of broad national power suggested in these early civil rights cases. The famous Slaughterhouse Cases, though not directly involving Negro rights, pointed the new direction. Denying that a Louisiana statute which created a monopoly in the slaughtering trade deprived several New Orleans butchers of rights of citizenship under the Fourteenth Amendment, the Supreme Court advanced the by now conventional view that American citizenship was dual. Fundamental civil rights pertaining to person and property were attributes of state citizenship, however, reasoned Justice Samuel F. Miller, while national citizenship, though it was primary and gave rise to state citizenship, consisted only in those few rights that arose from a citizen's direct and exclusive relationship with the federal government. Miller's principal finding, which was consistent with the original congressional understanding of 1866, was that under the Fourteenth Amendment the states had primary responsibility for protecting ordinary civil rights. Somewhat different was Miller's view of citizenship. While he did not refute the Republican doctrine of dual citizenship, he gave it a new gloss by treating national and state aspects as separate and exclusive rather than complementary and concentric.

More directly pertinent to blacks and the emerging law on civil rights was the Cruikshank decision of 1874. This case arose out of the Colfax massacre in Louisiana, and involved the indictment of about 100 whites under section 6 of the enforce-

32. Frantz, "Congressional Power to Enforce the Fourteenth Amendment," 1362–64; Kaczorowski, "The Nationalization of Civil Rights," 229–44.

ment act of 1870 for conspiring to deprive Negroes of their rights as United States citizens.[33] Justice Joseph P. Bradley in the Circuit Court in Louisiana held the indictment void on the ground that the enforcement act on which it was based exceeded the limits of congressional power under the Fourteenth Amendment. In Bradley's view the act operated directly on individuals, in the nature of a municipal ordinance superseding state law. Properly understood, said Bradley, the Fourteenth Amendment did not authorize federal legislation against ordinary crime, but only against denials of civil rights by states. Bradley added that this view of the amendment did not mean that Congress could under no circumstances legislate directly on individuals. Should it do so, however, its action must be based on state denial of civil rights—either by commission or omission—and its legislation must make this justification unequivocally clear. It was this that the act of May 1870 failed to do. Bradley observed in conclusion that Congress could deal with private discrimination only if it was motivated by racial rather than ordinary criminal intent, and only if states in their administration of ordinary criminal law denied equality to Negroes.[34]

Bradley's circuit court opinion narrowed the scope of the first enforcement act at a time when political pressures were seriously impeding federal civil rights efforts. When the Supreme Court took the Cruikshank case on appeal in 1876, pressure to abandon Reconstruction was stronger, and the Court's decision circumscribed federal authority even further. Declaring the government's indictment of the Colfax assailants invalid, Chief Justice Morrison R. Waite invoked the state action theory of the Fourteenth Amendment. Waite presented the theory, however, without the qualifications concerning legislation against private discrimination that Bradley had noted. The right of assembly which the Colfax Negroes claimed had been denied

33. The right to vote, assemble, bear arms, and receive protection in life, liberty, and property were identified as the national rights which had been denied.
34. U.S. v. Cruikshank, 25 *Federal Cases* 707 (1874); Frantz, "Congressional Power to Enforce the Fourteenth Amendment," 1366–68.

them, said Waite, was not an attribute of national but rather of state citizenship. Therefore it was improper for the federal government to seek an indictment for denial of this right. The indictment was further defective because it was directed against private rather than state action. The due process clause of the Fourteenth Amendment, Waite reasoned, did not enlarge the rights that one citizen enjoyed against another. Finally, Waite held that insofar as the indictment stated that the Colfax Negroes were denied the full benefit of all laws and proceedings for the protection of person and property (in accordance with the Civil Rights Act of 1866), it was invalid because it did not in express terms aver that the Colfax crimes were racially motivated.[35]

A second important case in 1876, U.S. v. Reese, established what few had doubted concerning the Fifteenth Amendment, namely, that it did not grant the right to vote and it was aimed at state actions that denied suffrage on racial grounds. The Court here threw out an indictment under the Enforcement Act of 1870 of a Kentucky election official for refusing to count a Negro's vote. The indictment was objectionable because the act on which it was based did not in express terms limit the offenses with which it was concerned to those motivated by racial discrimination. In other words, the Court thought the act tried to stop private interference with the right to vote in general rather than confining itself to state action that denied suffrage on racial grounds.[36]

The Reese and Cruikshank decisions were followed by the withdrawal of federal troops from the South after the election of 1876. Although for several years Republicans continued to use voting rights and federal aid to education in the South as political issues, the events of 1876 signaled the end of active federal intervention in southern civil rights policy. If they had not already, civil rights questions now took on a decidedly anticlimac-

35. Ibid., 1370–73; C. Peter Magrath, *Morrison R. Waite: The Triumph of Character* (New York, 1963), 126–27.
36. U.S. v. Reese, 92 *U.S.* 214 (1876); Swinney, "Enforcing the Fifteenth Amendment," 208; Magrath, *Morrison R. Waite,* 128–29.

tic character as the federal judiciary accommodated itself to the political currents that brought Reconstruction to an end.

In the cases of 1876 the Supreme Court negated parts of the Enforcement Act of 1870; not until the case of U.S. v. Harris in 1882 did the Court apply similar strictures to the Ku Klux Act of 1871. Using the familiar state action argument, the Court threw out an indictment of twenty white Tennesseans for depriving Negro citizens of the equal protection of the laws. The Fourteenth Amendment authorized Congress to legislate only against state action, the Court reasoned, but the act of 1871 failed to express this understanding. It was not framed, said Justice William B. Woods, so as to take effect only after it was clear that states had denied civil rights, but rather punished private wrongs irrespective of state efforts in enforcing civil rights. Woods's opinion allowed of the inference that Congress might legislate against private discrimination when states were remiss in protecting citizens' rights. Bradley had made this point in his Cruikshank circuit court opinion, and, though it was of secondary importance, it had entered into congressional thinking in the civil rights settlement of 1866. In the political circumstances of the 1880's, however, this inference was hardly a source of encouragement to advocates of federal civil rights protection.[37]

In 1883 the Supreme Court reaffirmed the state action theory of the Fourteenth Amendment in a major decision invalidating the Civil Rights Act of 1875. This measure, which declared that all persons were entitled to the full and equal enjoyment of public accommodations in inns, transportation facilities, and places of amusement, and which punished any person who denied equal access in these places, was more the product of political maneuvering than any serious civil rights concern.[38] The act is of interest nonetheless for showing how Republicans again went to the limit of the civil rights settlement of 1866, yet

37. U.S. v. Harris, 106 *U.S.* 629 (1882).
38. Bertram Wyatt-Brown, "The Civil Rights Act of 1875," *Western Political Quarterly*, XVIII (December 1965), 763–75.

remained within its scope. To be sure, the act can be read as a radical attempt to prohibit private discrimination in patent disregard of the state action limitation. Republican congressmen, however, based the act rather on the idea that citizens had equal rights in institutions created or regulated by law, or in which the state was substantially involved. They did not believe it would apply to strictly private businesses, but only to those, in the nature of public utilities, which enjoyed monopolistic privileges or occupied a special position by virtue of their legal franchise.[39]

From the moment of its passage there was widespread resistance to the Civil Rights Act of 1875, and at best desultory enforcement by federal authorities while awaiting judicial review of the measure.[40] In the Civil Rights Cases of 1883 the Supreme Court finally offered its verdict.

The Court declared the 1875 measure an unconstitutional attempt to punish strictly private discrimination. The act encroached upon state municipal law, explained Justice Bradley, and violated the Fourteenth Amendment requirement that federal legislation be limited to correcting state action that denied civil rights. As in earlier opinions, Bradley recognized the possibility of federal legislation punishing private individuals on a showing of state failure to protect citizens against private wrongs. While this offered a theoretical avenue for federal redress, in the contemporary political situation it was irrelevant. Bradley reflected a public opinion grown weary of the Negro question in concluding that the Thirteenth Amendment, on which the government had also based its defense of the Civil Rights Act of 1875, did not prohibit the kinds of private discrimination which the act sought to proscribe. Discrimination, in other words, was not a badge or incident of slavery, but an

39. Alfred Avins, "The Civil Rights Act of 1875: Some Reflected Light on the Fourteenth Amendment and Public Accommodations," *Columbia Law Review*, LXVI (May 1966), 873–915.

40. John Hope Franklin, "Enforcement of the Civil Rights Act of 1875," *Prologue*, VI (Winter 1974), 225–35.

ordinary crime under the jurisdiction of the states.[41] Thus the Supreme Court gave scope to private actions in the civil rights field, just as in the sphere of economic relationships in general during the 1880s and 1890s it gave wide latitude to private conduct under the doctrine of liberty of contract.[42]

Although the Supreme Court took a narrow view of the civil rights acts of the 1870s, its affirmation of the state action limitation on congressional power and its moderate interpretation of the effect of the Reconstruction amendments on federal-state relations generally agreed with the constitutional settlement of 1866. Certainly the Court rejected the radical view that the Fourteenth Amendment made national citizenship the exclusive source of fundamental civil rights and gave Congress power to legislate against violations of civil rights from whatever source. But the framers of the Fourteenth Amendment had of course denied this view also. Equally important, the Court rejected the conservative contention that under the Fourteenth Amendment Congress could legislate only against overt, positive state action that denied civil rights.

The trouble with the enforcement acts of the 1870s was that they did not clearly express the idea that the failure of the states to protect civil rights provided the constitutional justification for punishing individual private wrongs. This failure on the part of the states was so egregious that Republican lawmakers took it for granted and made it the unspoken assumption on which their legislation rested. The measures did not, that is, in express terms declare that inability or unwillingness to secure equal rights constituted a form of state action that Congress could correct. This defect has been variously attributed to poor legislative drafting and to the fact that lawmakers working in such

41. Civil Rights Cases, 109 *U.S.* 3 (1883); John Anthony Scott, "Justice Bradley's Evolving Concept of the Fourteenth Amendment from the Slaughterhouse Cases to the Civil Rights Cases," *Rutgers Law Review*, XXV (Summer 1971), 552–70.

42. Ira Nerken, "A New Deal for the Protection of Fourteenth Amendment Rights: Challenging the Doctrinal Bases of the *Civil Rights Cases* and State Action Theory," *Harvard Civil Rights/Civil Liberties Law Review*, XII (Spring 1977), 297–316.

unfamiliar legal territory did not know how to solve the inherently difficult problem of protecting against racially motivated civil rights violations while avoiding substantial invasion of states' municipal jurisdiction.[43] It seems likely too that pressure caused by the waning of radicalism and the growth of Klan violence made Republicans politically desperate and therefore careless in their legislative efforts in the enforcement acts.[44]

Although he did not carry the Court with him on this point, Justice Joseph P. Bradley in 1874 advanced a theory of national protection of civil rights that accurately reflected the original congressional outlook of 1866. Bradley distinguished between categorical rights such as making contracts and buying property, which attached to American citizenship in general, and private rights of individuals under state law, which in specific situations guaranteed the right to make this contract or purchase that piece of property.[45] Consisting figuratively in an outer circle of national and an inner circle of state citizenship, this concept found expression in the Civil Rights Act of 1866, the Fourteenth Amendment, and the Ku Klux Act of 1871. The latter two measures especially referred to general rights such as equal protection of the law and equal privileges and immunities. Yet the Supreme Court in the Slaughterhouse and Cruikshank cases gave a different gloss to the doctrine of citizenship and viewed the state and national aspects of general American citizenship as separate and exclusive. While this outlook was not entirely erroneous, since certain rights did pertain peculiarly to the citizen's relationship with the federal government, it missed the point that national citizenship consisted in fundamental civil rights that were to be implemented in the sphere of state law, with the federal government acting as ultimate guarantor.

Although the Supreme Court rejected what might be called

43. Avins, "The Ku Klux Act of 1871," 379; Kaczorowski, "The Nationalization of Civil Rights," 186–88.
44. William Gillette, "Anatomy of a Failure: Federal Enforcement of the Right to Vote in the Border States during Reconstruction," in Curry, ed., *Radicalism, Racism, and Party Realignment*, 302–3.
45. Kaczorowski, "The Nationalization of Civil Rights," 302–3.

the concentric theory of American citizenship, it accepted without question other aspects of the civil rights settlement of 1866. The most important single issue in the civil rights question, the problem that seemed most urgent at the beginning of Reconstruction, was to prevent states from discriminating by race in their laws and policies. The framers of the Fourteenth Amendment insisted on the same law for black and white, and the Supreme Court agreed with this requirement. It found a state law limiting jury duty to whites to be in conflict with the equal protection clause of the Fourteenth Amendment; declared the action of a state judge in excluding blacks from jury service a violation of the Civil Rights Act of 1875; and held that although the laws and constitution of a state did not exclude blacks, the exclusion of Negroes from jury service by actual state practice was a denial of equal protection under the Fourteenth Amendment.[46]

The Supreme Court also recognized national power to protect political rights. In the early 1870s lower federal courts adopted the view that the right to vote in federal elections derived from state constitutions and laws. In Ex Parte Yarbrough in 1884, however, the Supreme Court declared that voters in national elections owed their right of suffrage to the federal Constitution, although it was necessary to consult state constitutions and laws to ascertain the qualifications of electors.[47] In the Yarbrough case the Court also upheld the Enforcement Act of 1870 against private individuals who deprived Negroes of the civil right of voting in a congressional election. In another case, invoking the power of Congress to regulate the time, place, and manner of elections, the Supreme Court applied the 1870 law against state officers who had perpetrated electoral fraud.[48] While these decisions hardly reversed the retreat from Recon-

46. Strauder v. West Virginia 100 *U.S.* 303 (1880); Ex parte Virginia, 100 *U.S.* 347 (1880); Neal v. Delaware, 103 *U.S.* 370 (1880).
47. Richard Claude, *The Supreme Court and the Electoral Process* (Baltimore, 1970), 28–31.
48. Ex parte Siebold, 100 *U.S.* 371 (1880).

struction, they serve as a reminder that Republican civil rights policy extended national power in important respects.

Together the voting rights and jury service cases show that the end of Reconstruction did not leave constitutional questions of civil rights in their antebellum condition. Indeed civil rights problems scarcely existed before the war, the extension of slavery then being the all-consuming, transcendent issue. By the 1880s, however, civil rights formed a part of constitutional politics, even if political circumstances in the late nineteenth century caused it to be subordinated in national politics and made further progress and change exceedingly difficult. In the words of anonymous Negro legal commentators in 1889, a "civil-rights man" had come into existence.[49]

Moreover a constitutional compromise had taken hold in general accordance with the moderate outlook of Reconstruction planners and civil rights advocates in 1866. National power over personal liberty and civil rights reached far beyond pre-1860 limits, through the operation of the Thirteenth, Fourteenth, and Fifteenth Amendments, the Civil Rights Act of 1866, and the enforcement acts of the 1870s, important parts of which remained in the United States code. On the other hand, the constitutional changes had considerably reduced state power over civil rights. No longer were the states autonomous in this critically important sphere of political life. Nevertheless, while a nationalization of civil rights had occurred, only to a limited extent did this process follow the course of centralization. The essential point about national civil rights policy during Reconstruction was that Republicans established minimum national standards for state civil rights policies.[50] States retained primary power and responsibility to regulate civil rights, but national civil rights standards now existed in the Constitution, and the federal government possessed concurrent power and ultimate responsibility to guarantee the rights of American citizens.

49. Hyman, *A More Perfect Union*, 273.
50. Daniel J. Elazar, "Civil War and the Preservation of American Federalism," *Publius*, I, no. 1, pp. 39–58.

As at the founding of the republic, the price of Union continued to be compromise, and the essence of the compromise still consisted in the peculiar idea of federalism which regarded states' rights and local self-government as the truest and most effective expression of American nationality.

6

The Significance
of Reconstruction

THE CIVIL WAR and Reconstruction marked a decisive phase in the nationalization of American life. During the American Revolution a national government had come into existence in advance of the social, cultural, and psychological attitudes that ordinarily sustain modern nationalism and nation-building. In a reversal of the usual pattern, the political structure that the Revolutionary crisis necessitated stimulated the growth of national identity and consciousness.[1] Through the first half of the nineteenth century cultural, social, and economic forces promoted the nationalization of American life and, despite vast diversity, encouraged a growing spirit of American nationality. Sectional and local attitudes also flourished, but there was nothing inconsistent about this development; multiple loyalties are by no means necessarily conflicting loyalties.

Yet in one important respect the tendency toward uniformity and integration that appeared in other aspects of American activity was notably absent. Distrusting centralization, Americans in their political and constitutional development emphasized local control, with the result that a polity in which, by original constitutional design, power was balanced, dispersed, and limited became in the nineteenth century even more decentralized. Under the states' rights outlook of Jeffersonian and Jacksonian democracy, and then under the proslavery state sov-

1. Yehoshua Arieli, *Individualism and Nationalism in American Ideology* (Baltimore, 1966) 29–46 and passim.

ereignty doctrine, states gained and the federal government lost power. Here indeed a distinct paradox appeared: the growth of nationalizing social and cultural attitudes amid political events —culminating in secession—that threatened the very existence of the national government.

The Civil War settled the question of whether the Americans as a national people had an authentic national government. In political and constitutional development the war produced significant nationalizing changes, in activities as varied as the banking business and the administration of justice in federal courts. A greater degree of centralization in policy making and administration did not, however, create a unitary national state. In fact wartime exigencies strengthened federalism, and in some respects led to an expansion of state as well as national power.[2] Against the disintegrative effects of state sovereignty, the Republican party which controlled the Union government asserted a state-rights nationalism. Insisting on federal guarantees of state performance in fields such as civil rights, Republicans yet regarded the states as the vital engines of republican government. The vigorous efforts of the states to regulate economic and social change in the years after Reconstruction depended upon this continued reliance on the federal principle of local control.[3] Indeed a century later the United States would appear in comparative perspective as an integrated modern society with a political and constitutional system still peculiarly pre-modern in its insistence on dividing, balancing, and limiting power, in accordance with the principles of federalism and the separation of powers.[4]

The abolition of slavery which resulted from the war also gave rise to significant nationalization in American life. Black people became citizens with national rights that entitled them to

2. Harold M. Hyman, *A More Perfect Union: The Impact of the Civil War and Reconstruction on the Constitution* (New York, 1973), 307–46.

3. See Morton Keller, *Affairs of State: Public Life in Late Nineteenth Century America* (Cambridge, Mass., 1977).

4. Samuel P. Huntington, "Political Modernization: America vs. Europe," *World Politics*, XVIII (April 1966), 378–414.

equality before the law in the states in which they resided. Neither a subnational group nor a legally distinct class, blacks began to achieve integration into the society on the basis of legal equality. Although racial prejudice remained strong, when Reconstruction ended, the principle of civil and political equality remained part of American public law.

Dramatic gains in the civil rights movement in the mid-twentieth century demonstrated that the legal injunction of equality before the law in the 1860s was but a starting point and that it failed to eliminate deeply ingrained discriminatory social practices. These recent changes in race relations, amounting to what has been called the second Reconstruction, have stimulated interest in the post-Civil War period, but they have had an unfortunate effect on historical interpretation insofar as they have been taken as incontestable evidence that the first Reconstruction failed. Many recent accounts of Reconstruction, assuming this conclusion at the outset, have accordingly made the analysis of failure their central concern.

Indeed a new historiographical orthodoxy has emerged which holds that Reconstruction failed because the concept of equality before the law, its central theoretical underpinning, was deeply flawed. According to the new orthodoxy, the advocates of equality before the law did not believe in racial equality, and the concept itself was inadequate because it did not extend beyond civil and political rights to the sphere of property and wealth. As a result black people were not integrated or accepted as equals, but remained a subordinate class as in slavery. Moreover bourgeois attachment to property kept Congress from confiscating and distributing land to the ex-slaves which would have made equality before the law meaningful by creating a foundation of economic democracy.[5]

5. Examples of this interpretation are numerous, as in Louis S. Gerteis, *From Contraband to Freedom: Federal Policy Toward Southern Blacks 1861–1865* (Westport, Conn., 1973); Staughton Lynd, ed., *Reconstruction* (New York, 1967); George M. Frederickson, *The Black Image in the White Mind: The Debate on Afro-American Character and Destiny, 1817–1914* (New York, 1971), 178–82; Kenneth M. Stampp,

As political argument this view might command attention, but it is unhistorical as an evaluation of the significance of Reconstruction. A fair appraisal must begin with an understanding of the purposes of postwar policy and an appreciation of the limiting circumstances and political realities in which it was pursued. The first and most fundamental aim was to restore the states to the Union, the second, to confirm emancipation and integrate the freedmen into the society. In this dual undertaking, civil rights laws and enforcement efforts were at once a political expedient and an ideological goal. Giving civil and political equality to blacks helped secure the power of the Republican party and the ascendancy of northern social and political institutions in the South. Yet equal rights for emancipated slaves could and sometimes did become an end in itself that was no less just for being expedient. It is pointless to try to determine which motive—justice or expediency—had the more important effect on events. The distinction in any case is a false one, not only because just or principled actions inevitably possess an instrumental character, but also because in a constitutional democracy action based on expediency, which after all refers to considerations of what is good, wise, or appropriate, are morally legitimate and proper.

While Reconstruction may appear inadequate when viewed from a twentieth-century perspective, in the context of nineteenth-century racial attitudes and political and constitutional ideas it was more success than failure. In the first place it confirmed emancipation and secured the civil liberty of the freed slaves. This result has usually been taken for granted, but it was actually more problematic than it appears in retrospect. In Maryland and other places, for example, an apprenticeship system of sizable proportions sprang up directly on the abolition of slavery. In 1865 Freedmen's Bureau and military authorities kept the system from spreading, and the federal circuit court

The Era of Reconstruction, 1865–1877 (New York, 1965). Cf. Herman Belz, "The New Orthodoxy in Reconstruction Historiography," *Reviews in American History*, I (March 1973), 106–13, for a more detailed analysis.

decision in the Turner case of 1867 brought about the release of over two thousand apprenticed black children.[6] The Black Codes of 1865–66 presented an equally serious attempt to compromise the freed slaves' civil liberty, but federal authorities abrogated these laws, and under the pressure of the second Freedmen's Bureau Act and the Civil Rights Act of 1866 southern states conferred a modicum of equal rights on the freed people. These changes were made slowly and reluctantly; Kentucky, for example, did not repeal its law excluding Negro testimony until 1872.[7] Nevertheless, southern states extended to blacks the same forms of due process and rules concerning trial and punishment that applied to whites.[8] The Klan crisis of the early 1870s again raised the question of elementary personal liberty and security, but national authorities effectively broke the organized violence of anti-Negro terrorist groups.

Enacting civil rights laws in situations of political crisis was one thing; enforcing them in a consistent and effective way, quite another. Although racial prejudice on the whole diminished in the Civil War era, it remained strong, so that after the Military Reconstruction Act of 1867 finally provided a way of restoring the Union, it was only a matter of time before the white southern majority, with the reluctant approval of the Republican party, regained effective control of local affairs. Still, race relations and federal-state relations were very different from antebellum times. Negroes were now national citizens with equal rights before state laws, and the states were no longer autonomous in matters of personal liberty and civil rights. Nor was equality before the law a mere formality. Blacks enjoyed a wide range of the most important ordinary rights, from owning property to acquiring an education to forming religious and community associations, that were denied them in slavery days.

6. Richard Paul Fuke, "A Reform Mentality: Federal Policy Toward Black Marylanders, 1864–1868," *Civil War History*, XXI (September, 1976), 224–25.

7. Victor B. Howard, "The Black Testimony Controversy in Kentucky," *Journal of Negro History*, LVIII (April 1973), 140–65.

8. George R. Bentley, *A History of the Freedmen's Bureau* (Philadelphia, 1955), 167.

It is true that former Confederates took up and vindicated the cause of white supremacy, but this step actually represented a significant change from the prewar southern desire to protect a distinctive if not necessarily separate civilization based on slavery. One tends to forget that at the end of the war most white southerners opposed any change in the status of Negroes; southern nationalism based on some form of coerced or unfree Negro labor continued to be a conceivable political object. After the Reconstruction Act of 1867, however, this kind of reactionism yielded to orthodox conservative Unionism, which accepted civil liberty and elementary civil rights for blacks.[9] Indeed the champions of white supremacy designed their appeal to compensate for the advance toward civil and political equality that blacks made during Reconstruction. Only if one regards slavery as in essence a form of racial control can one argue that emancipation brought no significant change in the status of blacks. Even then it would be a difficult argument to sustain. If slavery was primarily a matter of individual freedom, however, as contemporaries believed, then the conclusion is irresistible that blacks made significant gains during Reconstruction.

Under postwar sharecropping arrangements blacks continued to be agricultural laborers, in considerable degree subject to legal and economic controls that whites could manipulate. Yet sharecropping was profoundly different from and vastly superior to slavery as a form of labor. A compromise between the contract labor approach which planters preferred and the outright ownership or leasing of land to which the freedmen aspired, sharecropping offered blacks a significant degree of freedom. Aside from this politico-racial consideration, sharecropping made sense economically by redistributing risk between landlord and laborer and providing a stimulus for efficient production.[10] As for the enticement laws and other means

9. Jack P. Maddex, Jr., "Pollard's *The Lost Cause Regained:* A Mask for Southern Accommodation," *Journal of Southern History,* XL (November 1974), 595–612.

10. Joseph D. Reid, Jr., "Sharecropping as an Understandable Market Response: The Post-Bellum South," *Journal of Economic History* XXXIII (March 1973), 106–30.

of regulating black employment which appeared during Reconstruction and which have been described as involuntary servitude,[11] any system as fluid and flexible as these arrangements are conceded to have been, which permitted blacks to move about as they saw fit in relation to market conditions, was not involuntary servitude, at least not as contemporaries understood the term.

The establishment of racial segregation in the years following emancipation has seemed further evidence of the failure of Reconstruction. Yet compared to the customary treatment blacks had long received in social matters, namely, categorical exclusion, segregation was a decided gain. Before the war Negroes were excluded from schools, hospitals, militia companies, asylums, transportation facilities, and public accommodations generally. Southern whites attempted to maintain an exclusionary policy after the war, but they failed. Republican regimes in southern states insisted that institutions be opened to blacks, albeit on a segregated basis. In a decentralized and democratic political system in which racial and ethnic prejudice were strong forces, racial separation in the vaguely defined sphere of social relations that lay outside the area of civil and political equality was the most that could realistically be achieved. Blacks accepted segregation because it was better than exclusion and because it appealed to their sense of separate identity.[12]

If the introduction of segregation is not a reason for judging Reconstruction a failure, even less does the absence of a radical policy of land reform necessitate such a conclusion. To say that the struggle for civil and political equality produced no significant change because Congress did not provide the economic basis that would have made equality before the law more than an empty formality is to read back into the 1860s a favorite twentieth-century notion. Confiscation and land redistribution

11. William Cohen, "Negro Involuntary Servitude in the South: A Preliminary Analysis," *Journal of Southern History*, XLII (February 1976), 31–60.
12. Howard N. Rabinowitz, "From Exclusion to Segregation: Southern Race Relations, 1865–1890," *Journal of American History*, LXIII (September 1976), 325–50.

lacked anything like the kind of support needed to warrant the conclusion that Republicans missed a golden opportunity to make Reconstruction a success when they let President Johnson return southern plantations to their former rebel owners. One could argue on more persuasive grounds that Reconstruction failed because white Americans did not uphold professed ideals of Christian brotherhood and democratic fair play. These ideals at least found resonance in the society and served as a lever for realizing the goal of equality before the law. Only a very few radicals, on the other hand, thought private property should be given to the freedmen, and even Thaddeus Stevens's land redistribution bill did not propose to give land to the freedmen outright, but rather conveyed it to trustees for the use of the freedmen for a period of ten years.[13]

Considering the vast dimensions of the social change that emancipation produced and the habits of racial and ethnic prejudice that characterized the decentralized political system in the United States, it is remarkable that Republican congressmen were able to nationalize civil rights and lay the foundation for integrating the freed slaves on the basis of equality before the law. In a society that made citizenship the basis of nationality, and that rejected gradations of citizenship for a comprehensive recognition of equal rights for all members of the polity, antebellum slavery and racial prejudice had required the virtual dehumanization of black people, both slave and free. When emancipation occurred and opened a breach in the wall of racial prejudice, the American commitment to democracy, in conjunction with expedient political considerations, operated to include blacks as citizens of the nation.[14] From being fiercely exclusionist, American politics in a very short time became radically inclusionist in a racial sense.

The policy of racial inclusiveness, it is all too clear, did not

13. H.R. No. 63, December 20, 1865, File of Printed Bills of the U.S. Congress, Library of Congress. After ten years absolute title to the land was to go to the freedmen.
14. Louis Hartz, *The Founding of New Societies: Studies in the History of the United States, Latin America, South Africa, Canada, and Australia* (New York, 1964), 50, 101–3.

rest on a transformation of racial attitudes and fell woefully short in practice of what its most sanguine proponents hoped for. The significant point, however, is not that legal commitments "overreached moral persuasion,"[15] but that Republicans insisted on civil equality for blacks in spite of pervasive social prejudice. Though far less hostile toward Negroes than their Democratic opponents, most Republicans accepted the conventional nineteenth-century belief in Negro inferiority. Nevertheless, they wrote laws and instituted a policy aimed at making blacks equal citizens. "Human rights do not depend on the equality of Man or Races," the New York *Tribune* said in explanation of this policy, "but are wholly independent of them."[16] In the twentieth century precisely the opposite circumstance prevails: the principle of legal equality derives from a moral belief in the equality of all races. In the 1860s, in contrast, the principle of equal rights derived its legitimacy from the commitment to republican institutions. "Because I am an American citizen," declared Maryland Congressman John L. Thomas in 1866, "I choose to give [Negroes] what God has given me and every man," namely, the natural rights of civil liberty.[17]

It has become customary to say that these steps toward legal equality proved significant only in the long run, as a basis for the advances blacks made in the mid-twentieth century.[18] While it is true that the recent civil rights movement built on the foundations laid in the 1860s, it is not true that the significance of Reconstruction and the constitutional changes it produced lay only in the future. On the contrary, the civil rights laws and policies that Congress enacted had an unquestionably large im-

15. C. Vann Woodward, *The Burden of Southern History*, rev. ed. (New York, 1968), 66.

16. New York *Tribune*, October 7, 1862, quoted in Robert F. Durden, "Ambiguities in the Antislavery Crusade of the Republican Party," in Martin Duberman, ed., *The Antislavery Vanguard: New Essays on the Abolitionists* (Princeton, 1965), 390.

17. Quoted in Fuke, "A Reform Mentality," 234.

18. Cf. Stampp, *The Era of Reconstruction*, 214–15, and Robert Cruden, *The Negro in Reconstruction* (Englewood Cliffs, N.J., 1969), 167–68.

pact on all whom they affected, both black and white. Contemporaries did not doubt the practical significance of the new emphasis on equality before the law, nor fail to see that it was both the cause and consequence of major changes in southern society and American race relations. In that fact more than in events a century later lay the historical significance of Reconstruction.

A Bibliographical Review

IN THE PAST two decades historians have restored constitutional issues to a prominent place in Civil War and Reconstruction historiography. A century ago orthodox opinion viewed the Civil War preeminently as the result of conflict between the constitutional philosophies of states' rights and federal centralization. In the early twentieth century scholarly interest in social and economic history directed attention away from constitutionally oriented accounts of American history, including the history of the nation's most profound constitutional crisis. Although it expressed the entirely sound proposition that political ideas could not be understood apart from their social context, Civil War historian James G. Randall's assertion in 1926 that no issues were primarily constitutional in nature, and that constitutional and legal history were useful mainly for the light they threw on social history, reflected the decline of the field. Howard K. Beale epitomized this development when he wrote in 1930 that the constitutional arguments of the Civil War era were "pure shams" or "mere justification of practical ends" which determined nothing. Expediency, Beale concluded, was all that mattered in public affairs.

Even as he denied the significance of constitutional questions, however, Beale alluded to a fact that eventually provided the basis for the reassessment of constitutionalism in the Civil War era that has occurred in recent years. Constitutional arguments attracted attention, Beale observed, because "It was a day when constitutional theories were required for all practice." Starting with isolated studies of the Fourteenth Amendment in the late 1930s, constitutional historians have reconsidered the events of the Civil War and Reconstruction from the standpoint of the popular attitude underlying this requirement of constitutional rhetoric. They have recognized, in other words, that contemporaries cared deeply about the Constitution, regarding it not only as a reflection of fundamental social values but also as a guide to political action. The result has been a renewed interest in the description of constitutional change in the Civil War era, and also a willingness to conclude that constitutional rules, beliefs, and attitudes which were taken seriously in these ways had an important impact on the actual course of events. In short, historians tend increasingly to include constitutional issues among the dynamic factors that shaped the major political developments of the period.

As usual in such matters, this shift in historical outlook appears to have arisen more out of contemporary political and social trends than the accumulation of new knowledge. In the reform era of the early twentieth century many scholars and intellectuals viewed the Constitution as a conservative instrument of class privilege and interest group advantage. Economic or material interests rather than political principles or ideas seemed to provide the most realistic explanation of political action. After the western democracies successfully resisted the challenge of totalitarianism in the crisis of World War II and the Cold War, however, students of history and politics more readily acknowledged the value of constitutionalism and the rule of law. In the 1950s and '60s the civil rights movement, which depended directly on constitutional amendments adopted in the Reconstruction period, further stimulated awareness of the practical importance of constitutionalism for social change. As people tried to apply constitutional principles in dealing with problems of racial discrimination, historians attributed to Americans in the 1860s an authentic concern for constitutionalism as part of their response to the twin crisis of disunion and the abolition of slavery. A review of some of the leading works on government and politics in the Civil War era will illustrate these changes in historical outlook.

The best general accounts of the Civil War and Reconstruction which give significant attention to constitutional matters are

Carl Russell Fish, *The American Civil War* (New York, 1937);
James G. Randall and David Donald, *The Civil War and Re-
construction* (2nd rev. ed., Boston, 1969); Allan Nevins, *The
War for the Union* (4 vols.; New York, 1959–71); and Peter
J. Parish, *The American Civil War* (New York, 1975). For
sustained constitutional analysis of a high order, William A.
Dunning, *Essays on the Civil War and Reconstruction* (rev. ed.,
New York, 1904), remains unrivaled. Thoughtful and judicious,
it reflects a moderately pro-southern point of view strongly
tempered by a sense of political realism. John W. Burgess, *The
Civil War and the Constitution* (2 vols.; New York, 1901), and
Reconstruction and the Constitution, 1866–1876 (New York,
1902), provide thorough narratives from a nationalist perspective. Writing at a time when constitutional analysis was the
generally accepted way of examining public affairs, Dunning
and Burgess were as much political scientists as historians and
as a result their work possesses a certain richness of insight not
often found in later works. James G. Randall, *Constitutional
Problems Under Lincoln* (Urbana, Ill., 1926; rev. ed., 1951),
offers penetrating essays on a wide variety of constitutional and
legal topics. Long the standard work in Civil War constitutional
history, it has recently been supplemented in a significant way
by Harold M. Hyman, *A More Perfect Union: The Impact of
the Civil War and Reconstruction on the Constitution* (New
York, 1973). These two books deal with different questions for
the most part, but the chief difference between them lies in their
conception of constitutional history. As indicated above, Randall thought constitutional developments important insofar as
they reflected social history, while Hyman views constitutional
issues and ideas as having a dynamic, motivating effect. Hyman's writings have done much to place constitutional history
once again in the mainstream of Civil War scholarship, but
perhaps the most important single work in this respect has been
Arthur Bestor's fine essay, "The American Civil War as a Constitutional Crisis," *American Historical Review*, LXIX (January 1964), 327–52. Concerned ultimately with elucidating the
nature of historical explanation, Bestor employs the concept of

the configurative effect of constitutions to show that constitutional issues are indeed real issues.

Several works deal with the closely related questions of federalism, Unionism, and nationalism. Yehoshua Arieli, *Individualism and Nationalism in American Ideology* (Cambridge, Mass., 1964), describes the context of political and social philosophy in which particular constitutional points of view developed between the Revolution and the Civil War. Illuminating if demanding analyses of northern Unionism may be found in Paul C. Nagel, *One Nation Indivisible: The Union in American Thought, 1776–1861* (New York, 1964), and Major L. Wilson, *Space, Time, and Freedom: The Quest for Nationality and the Irrepressible Conflict, 1815–1861* (Westport, Conn., 1974). David M. Potter, "The Historian's Use of Nationalism and Vice Versa," in Don E. Fehrenbacher, ed., *History and American Society: Essays of David M. Potter* (New York, 1973), subjects southern nationalism to critical scrutiny, while Arthur Bestor, "State Sovereignty and Slavery: A Reinterpretation of Proslavery Constitutional Doctrine, 1846–1860," *Journal of the Illinois State Historical Society*, LIV (Summer 1961), 117–80, concludes that centralizing power rather than local self-determination was the main theme of southern political thought. Valuable older works include Andrew C. McLaughlin, "Social Compact and Constitutional Construction," *American Historical Review*, V (April 1900), 467–90; Jesse T. Carpenter, *The South as a Conscious Minority, 1789–1861* (New York, 1930); Roy F. Nichols, "Federalism *versus* Democracy: The Significance of the Civil War in the History of United States Federalism," in *Federalism as a Democratic Process: Essays by Roscoe Pound, Charles H. McIlwain, and Roy F. Nichols* (New Brunswick, 1942); Charles M. Wiltse, "From Compact to National State in American Thought," in M. Konvitz and A. Murphy, eds., *Essays in Political Theory, Presented to George H. Sabine* (Ithaca, 1948). Republicanism, which has been thoroughly studied in its eighteenth century origins, in its nineteenth century development is the subject of Harry V. Jaffa, *Crisis of the House Di-*

vided: An Interpretation of the Issues in the Lincoln-Douglas Debates (New York, 1959); Eric Foner, *Free Soil, Free Labor, Free Men: The Ideology of the Republican Party before the Civil War* (New York, 1970); William M. Wiecek, *The Guarantee Clause of the U.S. Constitution* (Ithaca, 1972); and George M. Dennison, *The Dorr War: Republicanism on Trial* (Lexington, 1976).

The growth of presidential power of course forms a major aspect of Civil War constitutional history. Dunning offers a concise introduction to the problem of constitutional dictatorship in his *Essays on the Civil War and Reconstruction*. Edward S. Corwin, *The President: Office and Powers, 1787–1957* (New York, 1957); Wilfred E. Binkley, *President and Congress* (New York, 1962); Clinton L. Rossiter, *Constitutional Dictatorship: Crisis Government in the Modern Democracies* (Princeton, 1948); and K. C. Wheare, *Abraham Lincoln and the United States* (London, 1948), provide able brief accounts of Lincoln's presidency. Interpretive works which present a favorable assessment of Lincoln's constitutionalism are Andrew C. McLaughlin, "Lincoln, the Constitution, and Democracy," *International Journal of Ethics*, XLVII (October 1936), 1–24; James G. Randall, "The Rule of Law Under Lincoln," in *Lincoln the Liberal Statesman* (New York, 1947); and Morgan D. Dowd, "Lincoln, the Rule of Law and Crisis Government: A Study of his Constitutional Law Theories," *University of Detroit Law Journal*, XXXIX (June 1962), 633–49. William B. Hesseltine, *Lincoln and the War Governors* (New York, 1948); Gottfried Dietze, *America's Political Dilemma: From Limited to Unlimited Democracy* (Baltimore, 1968); and Robert M. Spector, "Lincoln and Taney: A Study in Constitutional Polarization," *American Journal of Legal History*, XV (July 1971), 199–214, criticize Lincoln's concentration of power in the federal executive. Useful treatments of Lincoln's politico-constitutional thought are T. Harry Williams, "Abraham Lincoln— Principle and Pragmatism in Politics: A Review Article," *Mississippi Valley Historical Review*, XL (June 1953), 89–106; James A. Rawley, "The Nationalism of Abraham Lincoln,"

Civil War History, IX (September 1963), 283–98; and David Donald, "Abraham Lincoln: Whig in the White House," in *Lincoln Reconsidered: Essays on the Civil War Era* (New York, 1961). Edmund Wilson, *Patriotic Gore: Studies in the Literature of the American Civil War* (New York, 1962), contains a brilliant essay on the religious and mystical aspects of Lincoln's Unionism. The most valuable studies of Lincoln's attitude and actions toward blacks are Ludwell H. Johnson, "Lincoln and Equal Rights: The Authenticity of the Wadsworth Letter," *Journal of Southern History*, XXXII (February 1966), 83–87; Harold M. Hyman, "Lincoln and Equal Rights for Negroes: The Irrelevancy of the 'Wadsworth Letter,' " *Civil War History*, XII (September 1966), 258–66; Robert F. Durden, "A. Lincoln: Honkie or Equalitarian?" *South Atlantic Quarterly*, LXXI (Summer 1972); 280–91; Don E. Fehrenbacher, "Only His Stepchildren: Lincoln and the Negro," *Civil War History*, XXII (December 1974), 293–310; George M. Fredrickson, "A Man But Not a Brother: Abraham Lincoln and Racial Equality," *Journal of Southern History*, XLI (February 1975), 39–58.

Lincoln's passive, Whiggish attitude toward nonmilitary matters allowed significant constitutional developments to take place outside of the executive branch. Harold M. Hyman casts fresh light on many of these developments in several works, including *Era of the Oath: Northern Loyalty Tests during the Civil War and Reconstruction* (Philadelphia, 1954); *Stanton: The Life and Times of Lincoln's Secretary of War,* with Benjamin P. Thomas (New York, 1962); "Reconstruction and Political-Constitutional Institutions: The Popular Expression," in Hyman, ed., *New Frontiers of the American Reconstruction* (Urbana, 1966); "Law and the Impact of the Civil War: A Review Essay," *Civil War History*, XIV (March 1968), 51–59; *A More Perfect Union: The Impact of the Civil War and Reconstruction on the Constitution.* Leonard P. Curry, *Blueprint for Modern America: Nonmilitary Legislation of the First Civil War Congress* (Nashville, 1968), describes legislative activism in great detail, while Donald G. Morgan examines congressional determination of constitutional questions during the Civil War in *Congress and the Constitution: A Study of Responsibility* (Cambridge, Mass., 1966). Patricia L. M. Lucie, "Confiscation: Constitutional Crossroads," *Civil War History*, XXIII (December 1977), 307–21, offers acute insights into congressional attempts to deal with new constitutional problems raised by the war. Most useful for understanding legislative efforts to create emergency government during the war are the contemporary writings of William Whiting, *War Powers Under the Constitution of the United States* (43rd ed., Boston, 1871); Henry Winter Davis, *Speeches and Addresses* (New York, 1867); and Sidney George Fisher, *The Trial of the Constitution* (Philadelphia, 1862). Phillip S. Paludan, *A Covenant with Death: The Constitution, Law, and Equality in the Civil War Era* (Urbana, 1975), examines Fisher, Francis Lieber, and Joel Parker as exponents of wartime constitutionalism. W. H. Riker, "Sidney George Fisher and the Separation of Powers During the Civil War," *Journal of the History of Ideas*, XV (June 1954), 397–412, views Fisher as the advocate of congressional hegemony. The same theme informs T. Harry Williams's studies of executive-legislative relations, especially *Lincoln and the Radicals* (Madison, 1941), and "Lincoln and the Radicals: An Essay in Civil War History and Historiography," in Grady McWhiney, ed., *Grant, Lee, Lincoln and the Radicals: Essays on Civil War Leadership* (Evanston, 1964). Roy F. Nichols, *Blueprints for Leviathan: American Style* (New York, 1963), and James A. Rawley, *The Politics of Union* (Hinsdale, Ill., 1974), study wartime government and politics with special reference to Congress. The major institution of wartime emergency government by Congress is the subject of W. W. Pierson, Jr., "The Committee on the Conduct of the Civil War," *American Historical Review*, XXIII (April 1918), 550–76; T. Harry Williams, "The Committee on the Conduct of the War: An Experiment in Civilian Control," *Journal of the American Military Institute*, III (Fall 1939), 139–56; and Hans L. Trefousse, "The Joint Committee on the Conduct of the War: A Reassessment," *Civil War History*, X

(March 1964), 5–19. An illuminating study of northern political culture is Eric ᵀ. McKitrick, "Party Politics and the Union and Confederate War Efforts," in W. D. Burnham and W. N. Chambers, eds., *The American Party Systems: Stages of Political Development* (New York, 1967).

The relevant starting point for modern historiography on the policy of military emancipation is Richard Hofstadter's essay on Lincoln in *The American Political Tradition* (New York, 1948). In contrast to Hofstadter, who stresses the expedient nature of Lincoln's action, Mark L. Krug, "The Republican Party and the Emancipation Proclamation," *Journal of Negro History*, XLVIII (April 1963), 98–114, sees elements of idealism and social purpose in the policy of emancipation. Harry V. Jaffa, "The Emancipation Proclamation," in Robert A. Goldwin, ed., *100 Years of Emancipation* (Chicago, 1964), considers the wartime edict in relation to the original purposes of the Republican party in the 1850s. V. Jacque Voegeli, *Free But Not Equal: The Midwest and the Negro During the Civil War* (Chicago, 1967), is a superb account of Lincoln's gradual shift toward military emancipation. George M. Fredrickson, *The Inner Civil War: Northern Intellectuals and the Crisis of the Union* (New York, 1965), discusses the reaction of reformers to the Emancipation Proclamation. Legal aspects of emancipation receive attention in three interesting contemporary essays: James C. Welling, "The Emancipation Proclamation," *North American Review*, CXXX (February 1880), 163–85; R. H. Dana, Jr., "Nullity of the Emancipation Edict," *North American Review*, CXXXI (July 1880), 128–34; and Aaron A. Ferris, "The Validity of the Emancipation Edict," *North American Review*, CXXXI (December 1880), 551–76. Modern treatments of the subject include Randall, *Constitutional Problems Under Lincoln*; and Herman Belz, *A New Birth of Freedom: The Republican Party and Freedmen's Rights, 1861–1866* (Westport, 1976). That federal authorities kept freed blacks in an oppressed status after emancipation is the thesis of several recent works, including C. Peter Ripley, *Slaves and Freedmen in Civil War Louisiana* (Baton Rouge, 1976); and Louis S. Gerteis, *From Contraband to Freedman: Federal Policy Toward Southern Blacks, 1861–1865* (Westport, 1973). The same subject is treated more judiciously in Nevins, *The War for the Union*; James M. McPherson, *The Struggle for Equality: Abolitionists and the Negro in the Civil War and Reconstruction* (Princeton, 1964); Willie Lee Rose, *Rehearsal for Reconstruction: The Port Royal Experiment* (Indianapolis, 1964); and W. E. B. DuBois, *Black Reconstruction in America, 1860–1880* (New York, 1935). Forrest G. Wood, *Black Scare: The Racist Response to Emancipation and Reconstruction* (Berkeley, 1968), and George M. Fredrickson, *The Black Image in the White Mind: The Debate on Afro-American Character and Destiny, 1817–1914* (New York, 1971), describe the climate of racial attitudes in which post-emancipation policy developed.

Several works written in the 1960s present a favorable view of Congressional reconstruction. Eric L. McKitrick, *Andrew Johnson and Reconstruction* (Chicago, 1960), shifts the burden of responsibility for the breakdown in executive-legislative relations in 1866 from the radical Republicans to Johnson, and perceptively instructs historians on the relevance of constitutional theory in the struggle over reconstruction, W. R. Brock, *An American Crisis: Congress and Reconstruction, 1865–1867* (New York, 1963), and LaWanda Cox and John H. Cox, *Politics, Principle, and Prejudice, 1865–1866: Dilemma of Reconstruction America* (New York, 1963), underscore the Republican concern for civil rights. Herman Belz, *Reconstructing the Union: Theory and Policy during the Civil War* (Ithaca, 1969), deals with the origins of planning to restore the Union, while Ludwell H. Johnson, "Lincoln's Solution to the Problem of Peace Terms, 1864–1865," *Journal of Southern History*, XXXIV (November 1968), 576–86, emphasizes the politically conservative character of Lincoln's approach to reconstruction. Hyman, *A More Perfect Union*; Michael Les Benedict, *A Compromise of Principle: Congressional Republicans and Reconstruction, 1863–1869* (New York, 1974); and Paludan, *A Covenant with Death*, analyze the tension between Republicans' attachment to federalism and their desire to protect civil rights. Daniel J. Elazar, "Civil War and the Preservation of Federalism," *Publius*, I (1970), 39–58, refutes the notion that the war produced centralization of government. Michael Perman, *Reunion Without Compromise: The South and Reconstruction, 1865–1868* (Cambridge, U.K., 1973), shows Republican reluctance to deny local self-determination to southerners. Within the framework of federalism the powers of the national government nevertheless expanded. William M. Wiecek, "The Reconstruction of Federal Judicial Power, 1863–1875," *American Journal of Legal History*, XIII (October 1969), 333–59; Stanley I. Kutler, *Judicial Power and Reconstruction Politics* (Chicago, 1968); and J. David Hoeveler, Jr., "Reconstruction and the Federal Courts: The Civil Rights Act of 1875," *The Historian*, XXXI (August 1969), 604–17, describe the significantly broader jurisdiction of federal courts that existed by the end of Reconstruction. Morton Keller, *Affairs of State: Public Life in Late Nineteenth Century America* (Cambridge, Mass., 1977), stresses the emergence of active, reformist government at both the federal and state level during and immediately after the war.

A generation ago pioneering steps toward a reassessment of Civil War constitutionalism were taken in Howard Jay Graham, "The 'Conspiracy Theory' of the Fourteenth Amendment," *Yale Law Journal*, XLVII (January 1938), 371–403, XLVIII (December 1938), 171–94, and "The Early Anti-Slavery Backgrounds of the Fourteenth Amendment," *Wisconsin Law Review*, XXIII (1950), 479–507 (reprinted in Graham, *Everyman's Constitution: Historical Essays on the Fourteenth Amendment, the "Conspiracy Theory," and American Constitutionalism* [Madison, 1968]); Louis B. Boudin, "Truth and Fiction about the Fourteenth Amendment," *New York University Law Quarterly Review*, XVI (November 1938), 19–82; and Jacobus ten Broek, *The Anti-Slavery Origins of the*

Fourteenth Amendment (Berkeley, 1951; reprinted as *Equal Under Law* [New York, 1965]). In contending that the Thirteenth and Fourteenth Amendments were intended to revolutionize the federal system by creating national citizenship under plenary federal protection, these historians recalled the older work of Horace E. Flack, *The Adoption of the Fourteenth Amendment* (Baltimore, 1908). Alfred H. Kelly, "The Fourteenth Amendment Reconsidered: The Segregation Question," *Michigan Law Review*, LIV (June 1956), 1049–86, accepts the nationalist thesis, and Robert J. Kaczorowski amplifies it in "Searching for the Intent of the Framers of the Fourteenth Amendment," *Connecticut Law Review*, V (Winter 1973), 368–98. Arthur Kinoy, "The Constitutional Right of Negro Freedom," *Rutgers Law Review*, XXI (Spring 1967), 387–441, carries the nationalist idea to an interesting extreme. A more conservative interpretation of the Reconstruction amendments, which holds that national power to protect civil rights was limited by the state action theory, appears in Alexander Bickel, "The Original Understanding and the Segregation Decision," *Harvard Law Review*, LXIX (November 1955), 1–65; Laurent B. Frantz, "Congressional Power to Enforce the Fourteenth Amendment Against Private Acts," *Yale Law Journal*, LXXIII (July 1964), 1352–84; Alfred Avins, "The Ku Klux Act of 1871: Some Reflected Light on State Action and the Fourteenth Amendment," *St. Louis University Law Journal*, XI (1967), 331–81; Charles Fairman, *Reconstruction and Reunion, 1864–88: Part One* (New York, 1971); Michael Les Benedict, "Preserving the Constitution: The Conservative Basis of Radical Reconstruction," *Journal of American History*, LXI (June 1974), 65–90; and Belz, *A New Birth of Freedom*. In his usual provocative if narrowly legalistic manner, Raoul Berger reexamines the framing and application of the Fourteenth Amendment in *Government By Judiciary* (Cambridge, 1977). Joseph B. James's careful political study, *The Framing of the Fourteenth Amendment* (Urbana, 1956), provides a useful reminder that constitutional theory was by no means the concern of all members of Congress.

George R. Bentley, *A History of the Freedmen's Bureau* (Philadelphia, 1955), contains information about the Freedmen's Bureau courts, while Theodore B. Wilson, *The Black Codes of the South* (University, Ala., 1965), views postwar anti-Negro legislation as continuous with antebellum methods of racial control. Brock, *An American Crisis*; David Donald, *The Politics of Reconstruction, 1863–1867* (Baton Rouge, 1965); and Benedict, *A Compromise of Principle*, contain the best accounts of the Military Reconstruction Act of 1867. William Gillette, *The Right to Vote: Politics and the Passage of the Fifteenth Amendment* (Baltimore, 1965); and LaWanda Cox and John H. Cox, "Negro Suffrage and Republican Politics: The Problem of Motivation in Reconstruction Historiography," *Journal of Southern History*, XXXIII (August 1967), 303–30, discuss expediency versus principle in the adoption of the Fifteenth Amendment. Alfred Avins, "The Ku Klux Act of 1871: Some Reflected Light on State Action and the Fourteenth Amendment," is the most thorough analysis of that civil rights measure, and Everette Swinney, "Enforcing the Fifteenth Amendment, 1870–1877," *Journal of Southern History*, XXVIII (May 1962), 202–18, and William Gillette, "Anatomy of a Failure: Federal Enforcement of the Right to Vote in the Border States during Reconstruction," in Richard L. Curry, ed., *Radicalism, Racism, and Party Realignment: The Border States during Reconstruction* (Baltimore, 1969), describe the implementation of the enforcement acts generally in the 1870s. Richard Claude, *The Supreme Court and the Electoral Process* (Baltimore, 1970), traces the evolution of constitutional law concerning voting rights. The best general accounts of the Civil Rights Act of 1875 are Bertram Wyatt-Brown, "The Civil Rights Act of 1875," *Western Political Quarterly*, XVIII (December 1965), 763–75; Alfred H. Kelly, "The Congressional Controversy over School Segregation, 1867–1875," *American Historical Review*, LXIV (April 1959), 537–63; and John Hope Franklin, "Enforcement of the Civil Rights Act of 1875," *Prologue*, VI (Winter 1974), 225–35. For the judicial response to the civil rights measures of the 1870s, see Robert J. Harris, *The Quest for Equality: The Constitution, Congress, and the Supreme Court* (Baton Rouge, 1960); C. Peter Magrath, *Morrison R. Waite: The Triumph of Character* (New York, 1963); Michael J. Horan, "Political Economy and Sociological Theory as Influences Upon Judicial Policy-Making: The *Civil Rights Cases* of 1883," *American Journal of Legal History*, XVI (January 1972), 71–86; John Anthony Scott, "Justice Bradley's Evolving Concept of the Fourteenth Amendment from the Slaughterhouse Cases to the Civil Rights Cases," *Rutgers Law Review*, XXV (Summer 1971), 552–70; Ira Nerken, "A New Deal for the Protection of Fourteenth Amendment Rights: Challenging the Doctrinal Basis of the *Civil Rights Cases* and State Action Theory," *Harvard Civil Rights/Civil Liberties Review*, XII (Spring 1977), 297–366.

Otto H. Olson, "Southern Reconstruction and the Question of Self-Determination," in George M. Fredrickson, ed., *A Nation Divided: Problems and Issues of the Civil War and Reconstruction* (Minneapolis, 1975), and Herman Belz, "The New Orthodoxy in Reconstruction Historiography," *Reviews in American History*, I (March 1973), 106–13, question the assumption of several recent works that a more radical policy of land reform would have averted the failure of Reconstruction. Differing evaluations of the nature of Negro freedom and hence of Reconstruction are presented in William Cohen, "Negro Involuntary Servitude in the South, 1865–1940: A Preliminary Analysis," *Journal of Southern History*, XLII (February 1976), 31–60, and Howard N. Rabinowitz, "From Exclusion to Segregation: Southern Race Relations, 1865–1890," *Journal of American History*, LXIII (September 1976), 325–50. The most recent efforts to evaluate Reconstruction employ the methods of quantitative economic history and are reviewed in Harold D. Woodman, "Sequel to Slavery: The New History Views the Postbellum South," *Journal of Southern History*, XLIII (November 1977), 523–54.

As racial integration proceeds in contemporary American

society, historians will probably relate the history of Reconstruction more integrally to national history. The most satisfying and illuminating works which point in this direction are Hyman, *A More Perfect Union: The Impact of the Civil War and Reconstruction on the Constitution*, and Keller, *Affairs of State: Public Life in Late Nineteenth Century America*.

Index